MIGRATIONS

Bobby Tulloch

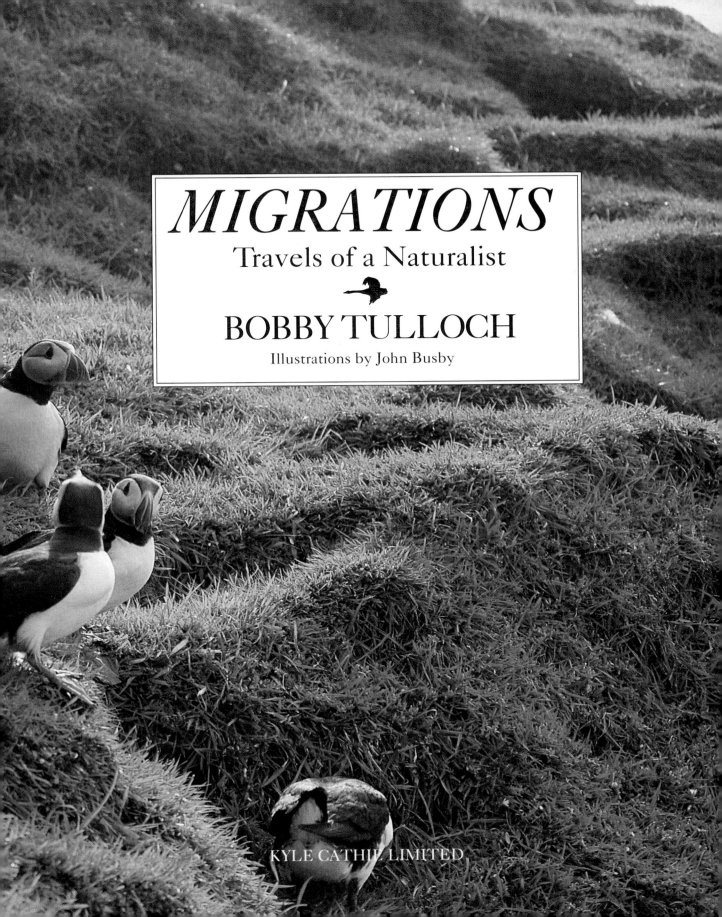

MIGRATIONS
Travels of a Naturalist

BOBBY TULLOCH

Illustrations by John Busby

KYLE CATHIE LIMITED

By the same author
Bobby Tulloch's Shetland

First published in Great Britain by
Kyle Cathie Limited
3 Vincent Square London SW1P 2LX

Text and photographs © copyright 1991 by Bobby Tulloch
Illustrations © copyright 1991 by John Busby

ISBN 1 85626 016 X

A CIP catalogue record for this book is available
from the British Library

Editor: Caroline Taggart
Designed by: Geoff Hayes
Printed and bound by: Printer Portuguesa Portugal

CONTENTS

1 THE WINTER SCENE

Grandfather used to say 'the day is a cock's stride longer at Old Newerday' (12th January), but in the first week of the new year there is little to show that the sun is creeping marginally higher each day. The earth is still fast in the grip of winter, and it will be weeks before there is any obvious sign that spring is not too far away.

But we humans are far too protected and insensitive nowadays to detect the subtleties of the earth's rhythms. It is well known in Shetland that the best of the fishing skippers of old had the ability to sense the correct course to steer in fog or darkness, by invoking a sort of 'sixth sense', and that it wasn't long after the invention of the compass before that ability faded and was lost for ever. The best we can hope for now is to see the effects on the wild birds and animals, whose behaviour is much more in tune with the seasons.

For a long time I have had a desire to understand better the behaviour and movements of wild birds and animals, and in the absence of the time (and probably the dedication) to undertake a proper study, I decided on a simple ploy which, I hoped, would get some results in the fullness of time. Accordingly, each week when I am at home, I take the car out and do a certain circuit, stopping at various vantage points where I can scan the surrounding area with binoculars or telescope, noting and memorising everything I see. In this way I hope eventually to get a better appreciation of the daily and seasonal lives of our local birds (and a few mammals).

I am not so naive as to expect a blinding flash of understanding, but bit by bit I think I am beginning to see patterns of behaviour, and even - in some cases - to recognise individuals. Of course there are disappointments and frustrations, but I find it fun!

Let's have a look, then, at my little circuit of friends just as the calendar tells us that a new year is dawning. . .

~

Dawn creeps reluctantly over the south-eastern horizon to outline the rounded grey hills and a lead-coloured sea. The 'front' warned for our area by the weathermen is still some kilometres away so, although high clouds have spread in from the west already, only a few little 'cats' paws' of wind ruffle the sea surface. 'If there's no wind

A view over Mid Yell voe.

Shetland starlings have been isolated for long enough to have developed racial characteristics. They are wider across the mandibles and have a more glossy, less spotted plumage than their mainland counterparts. Although we get thousands of immigrant starlings passing through, especially in autumn, they do not appear to get mixed up with the Shetland birds.

it's a fine day!' is a Shetland expression, and to me it is especially relevant because not only does it affect the movements of birds and animals, but it makes them so much easier to see on the water.

There was little need to hurry over breakfast, because even by nine o'clock there is barely enough light to see fine details, but shortly after nine the first starlings arrive for their morning meal, shoving and squabbling as they line up on the washing line to watch for the first human activity.

Our local starling population is a race apart in that they are non-migratory and have been isolated in the islands for long enough to have developed their own characteristics. They have wider bills than their mainland counterparts, and are also more glossy and less spotted.

One day I decided to test out these facts by catching and measuring some of our local birds. Catching them was a simple procedure of setting up a wire-mesh peat basket, held up at one side by a stick, with a string attached which led in through the window. A handful of scraps provided enough encouragement, and soon I was catching starlings in batches of up to a dozen. After taking a series of measurements I put a numbered ring on each bird's leg so that if one came to grief and was picked up at some time in the future, its identity could be established.

I didn't have long to wait for my first recovery, because the next day a kid arrived at the house carrying the ghastly yellow-coated corpse of a starling. 'This bird has a ring on its leg,' he informed me. Sure enough, it was one I had ringed less than 24 hours previously, and it had been found drowned in a bucket of custard! Apparently the school dessert hadn't been too popular with the children: the remains of the custard had been put out in a bin, and this had attracted that great opportunist, the starling.

From the batch of over seventy birds I ringed that day, only one other came to light. It was found dead - again at the school - almost ten years later to the day.

Many immigrant starlings pass through Shetland, particularly during the autumn migration period, but they seem not to mix with our birds - probably they don't even speak the same language!

As soon as dusk begins to fall, the local starlings begin to arrive at our house. They gather in noisy parties along the roof, on the chimney-pots and in the bushes in the garden. Then, as if at a given signal, they all take flight and head across the voe to their roosting places in the sea caves, where they spend the night, dry if not very warm!

The light has strengthened enough now to gather binoculars and telescope and start up the car for a look round my 'patch'. Come with me and see what we can find. . .

The first birds we see are a group of turnstones and a redshank, busily feeding in the park below the house, probing into the area of damaged grass where my neighbour's sheep are fed. The turnstones are winter visitors to Britain. They nest all round the shores of the Arctic and also on some islands in the Baltic. Although a few birds usually spend the summer in Shetland they have not so far been proved to breed here.

The redshank has vastly expanded its breeding range in Shetland in the last thirty years or so. I well remember the excitement of seeing the very first breeding pair on Yell back in the 1950s. Nowadays most suitable marshy areas attract one or more pairs.

It takes only a few minutes down to the shore, and I stop by the pier where one or two herring gulls are sitting rather listlessly, and a couple of hooded crows are poking about on the beach. The herring gulls are local resident birds, and great opportunists, able to change their feeding habits to whatever is available. When one or two local boats were fishing for 'whitefish' (principally haddock, whiting and cod) in the nearby inshore waters, they would be followed into port by a cloud of gulls, mainly herring and great black-backed gulls, who would clean up any leftover fish scraps.

But times change and the only locally based fishing-boats now fish for scallops, crabs and lobsters, none of which produce any offal or discards.

The new industry of salmon-farming has filled the gap as far as the scavenging gulls are concerned: the rearing cages are placed in the sheltered bays and 'sounds' between the islands and are fed on high-protein, manufactured food in pellet form, which are ferried out in sacks by small boats. The gulls (and to a lesser extent hooded crows and starlings) soon realised the value of this food supply, and quickly descend on any unattended sacks of salmon food left on the pier. The stout plastic sacks are ripped open by sharp beaks, allowing the birds to help themselves to the contents.

This is especially valuable to the birds in winter when supplies of 'natural' food are at a premium. Occasionally our local gulls will be joined by the odd glaucous gull whose summer home is farther north, in Iceland or even in Spitsbergen: the glaucous

Formerly a winter visitor to Shetland, since the last war redshanks have begun to breed regularly and to expand their range. Most suitable marshy areas now have noisy breeding pairs in summer. They lay four eggs in a well camouflaged nest.

gulls superficially resemble our herring gulls in that the adults have white bodies with grey backs, and the immatures are speckled brown, but at all ages they can be distinguished by having no black markings on the wing-tips, which are uniform fawn or white, depending on the age of the bird.

A ripple near the shore catches my eye and I swing the glasses quickly in case it is an otter - always a welcome sight! But it is merely a female red-breasted merganser searching for small fish in the shallows.

A bit of activity out on the water catches my attention next and I bring the 'scope out; it is a small party of long-tailed duck in their handsome winter plumage, the long tail-streamers of the drakes showing clearly as they display to the females. In spite of the temptation to get the car warmed up, I switch off the engine and wind down the window. Sure enough, I hear the lovely yodelling 'Cal-calloo' of the drake echoing across the water - surely one of the most evocative of the calls of our winter birds.

Time to leave the village now; I drive over the hill into the next valley, past brown winter hills scarred with peat diggings and with the occasional relief of green patches of sphagnum moss. Over the bridge, where brown, peaty water flows fast in winter spate. A raven flies past, looking dead black in the flat lighting, and croaks his way up the valley.

On to the main road, which runs through the island and, apart from the sheep

opposite: *Gulls are great opportunists, and are always on the outlook for new food sources - especially during the crucial winter period. They were quick to recognise the value of the highly concentrated 'pellet' food which is fed to farmed salmon and are always in attendance at feeding time in case of accidental spillage.*

below: *Long-tailed ducks breed in the far north with populations in places such as Iceland and northern Scandinavia. The usual nesting-places are near peaty pools on the tundra. In winter they migrate to inshore waters farther south, such as those of Shetland, Orkney and other coasts and islands in the north of Britain, where their loud 'yodelling' calls liven up the winter days.*

*King Eider duck and
Goldeneye duck.*

eking out a sparse living on the dead heather, there is little moving until I come to the head of Whalfirth, a long arm of the sea which pushes in from the west until it nearly cuts the island in half.

I stop at my usual vantage point and even before I have switched off the engine I see the otter. It is fishing about fifty metres offshore, flicking its tail as it dives, and staying under the water for only thirty seconds or so. It catches several eel-pout and a couple of butterfish which it eats on the surface, sometimes holding the fish between its forepaws in order to control their writhing. A few more dives and it surfaces with a larger fish which, judging from its colour, is a sea-scorpion.

This time the otter doesn't attempt to eat the fish in the water, but sets out purposefully for the shore, to disappear out of my view below the bank.

A heron appears, flapping ponderously across the voe and drops down beside a second bird I haven't seen, which is standing motionless in the shallows. A careful look with the glasses produces three more, hunched up in the shelter of the bank, looking introspective and a bit sad.

Herons generally breed in trees, which are lacking in Shetland, and these birds are almost certainly from Norway. Now and again a heron will fail to survive the rigours of winter, and occasionally dead birds have been found carrying a numbered metal ring on their leg. Invariably this has identified the bird as having been ringed as a nestling in Norway.

In their breeding haunts they will feed on frogs and small fish from the marshes and rivers. These habitats often freeze in winter; the coastline of western Norway has a very limited tidal range, and in any case the spectacular fiords usually plunge straight into the sea. So the birds have evolved the habit of flying a couple of hundred kilometres across to Shetland, where they can normally be assured of finding small fish around shorelines which never freeze over. They arrive in Shetland in late summer and spend the winter in lonely vigil along the sides of the voes. Those who

survive will head back across the North Sea about the month of March.

The light is quite reasonable by now, and the wind has increased to a gentle south-easterly, heralding the slow approach of the weather-front. But the sheltered voe is quite smooth. I can see several mergansers along the shores and, further out, a small party of goldeneye, the drakes unmistakable in black and white.

A very dark bird nearby makes me put up the 'scope again and I am surprised to find it is a common scoter, not at all common in Whalfirth Voe.

A couple of grey and white winter-plumage black guillemots - called tysties in Shetland - complete the picture, and I wind up the window and move on. The name tystie, which comes from the old Norse language, may refer to the birds' high-pitched, 'reedy' call.

There is quite a lot of activity as I come over the hill. The local rubbish-tip near the roadside is constantly picked over by gulls, starlings, crows and ravens. When I stop to check it out, a small flock of snow buntings fly up, upset by the watchful hooded crows.

Otters have been fully protected by the law for twenty years or so and have responded by becoming more tolerant of man's activities. They have been known to establish breeding holts under garage floors and even inside seldom-used outhouses. They have also taken advantage of the boulder break-waters at the car-ferry terminals and the oil-loading jetties at Sullom Voe.

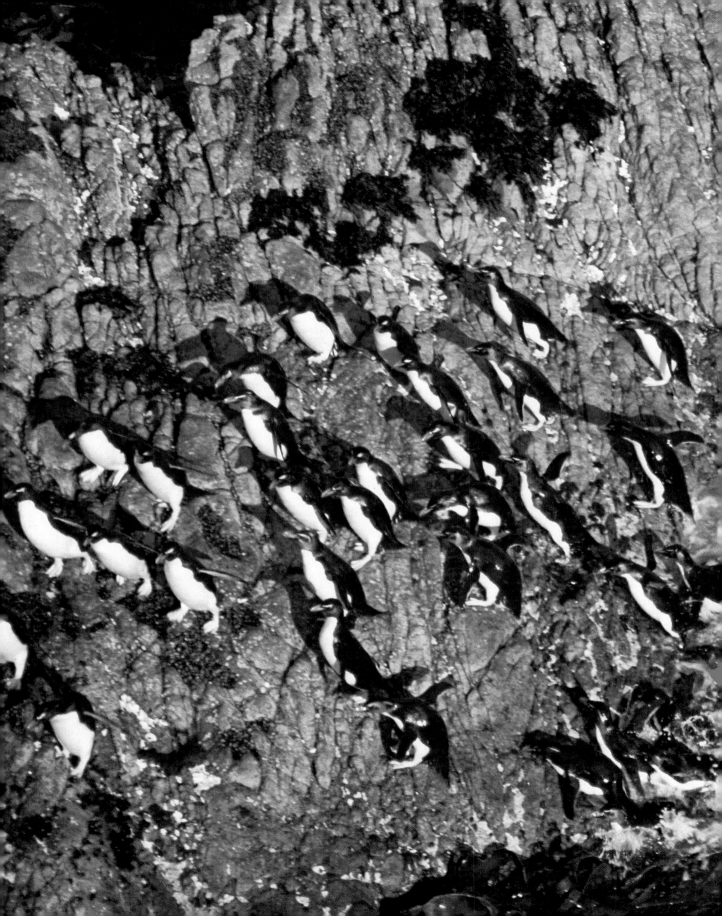

The small reedy pools nearby used to have a population of mallard, teal and black-headed gulls in summer as well as a pair of red-throated divers, but the hoodies have spoiled all that. They are wickedly mischievous. In idle moments or when there is not a lot going on on the dump, they fly across to annoy the birds on the pools. I have seen two crows gang up on a mallard with a brood of young, and, while one bird tormented the duck into chasing it, the other sneaked in and made off with a still struggling duckling in its beak. But if there are any duck here today they are well hidden in the soft rush which fringes the pools.

For a short run, I usually end at Westsandwick, taking the loop road through the township and back to the main road. The view from the top of the hill near Lungawater is worth the trip. Beyond the village, the island-dotted Yellsound is seen in all its variety of moods. It is very rarely still because of the strong tidal currents. These can throw up great 'overfalls' which small craft are well advised to avoid.

At the far side, the peninsula of Northmavine forms a boundary which ends at Fedeland, one of the famous 'haaf stations' of last century, from which the Shetland fisherman used to row or sail in open boats to the 'far haaf', the fishing grounds which could be as far as sixty or more kilometres from land. Now the routes of the haaf men are traversed by huge oil tankers en route to and from the large oil port of Sullom Voe.

Westsandwick has areas of fertile, sandy ground on which potatoes and oats are grown. After the crops have been harvested, there are good 'pickings' of seeds and insects for many birds. The first surprise is a party of fieldfares by the roadside which fly off 'chacking' among themselves. Are they recent arrivals from Norway, or birds which have been around since the autumn migration?

Puzzling over this, I nearly miss a water rail which scuttles off down a drainage ditch towards the loch of Westsandwick. I pull up and watch for a time but typically the bird does not re-appear. However, there is a pair of superb whooper swans on the loch, feeding by 'upending' to reach the vegetation on the bed. A pair of mallard and a lone wigeon are taking advantage of the weeds torn up by the swans, and a party of common gulls are bathing by the lochside.

Whooper swans are regular winter visitors to Shetland from their breeding

Winter flock of lapwings.

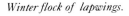

grounds in Iceland. They may build up to several hundred after arrival in September/October. But although there are hundreds of freshwater lochs in Shetland, the majority are on the acidic peatlands and do not produce enough underwater vegetation to satisfy the needs of big grazing birds like swans. So the whoopers tend to congregate on the lochs near the sea, many of which are fertilised by nutrients draining from the surrounding croft - and farmland. But even here, there is not enough to keep the swans in food all winter.

This winter has been relatively mild and frost free, so birds like lapwing and golden plover have delayed their departure south to the farms and coastal areas of Scotland and England, and many are still finding enough food in Shetland. Half a dozen lapwings are feeding on a potato field along with some sparrows and a party of twite, and I spot the white wing-flashes of a cock chaffinch among the black earth.

But best of all is a fine flock of over 150 golden plover which, along with a score of curlew, are feeding on the close-cropped turf of a hayfield near the churchyard. The curlew are probably local birds, but it is impossible to assess the status of the

A well-liked species is the 'snaa-fool' (snow-bird) which visits Shetland in the winter from the far north. These birds belong to the bunting family and in winter eat mainly seeds. In summer they feed their young mostly on insects.

plovers while they are in winter plumage and have lost their black 'shirt front'. The extent of these black markings varies according to latitude: the really dark birds breed in northern Iceland or Scandinavia. Golden plover are a widespread breeding bird in the summer, and whether this is a gathering of locals or birds from further north, I have no way of knowing.

But there it is, situation normal. There is no hint of any dramatic change in the standard winter scene. Out at sea things can be a lot more volatile. Storms and pollution, changes in food supplies, ocean currents and temperatures can all have drastic effects on those birds which spend their lives on the oceans of the world. But birds, with their great mobility, have evolved to cope with many of those problems.

But how is it for those birds which can't even fly, such as the penguins of the southern oceans? I am shortly to find out, for I am booked to fly out to the Falkland Islands in a few days!

Sanderlings sheltering in a high wind.

2 FALKLAND ISLANDS

Magellenic penguins.

However much you are attached to your own 'home ground', it is always exciting to visit new places, to see scenes that are different and, if you are a student of the natural world, to find birds and beasts that are 'new' and unfamiliar. To me there is an added dimension if that new country is of a similar type to my own habitat - islands.

I knew that the Falkland Islands were similar to Shetland in that both were a group of treeless islands in the middle of an ocean, and I wanted to see just how wild creatures - and birds in particular - had adapted as different species in what I imagined was a similar environment.

The conflict with Argentina in 1982 had brought the islands to the forefront of public awareness in Britain as never before. The building of a large new airport and the inauguration of twice-weekly flights from Britain had removed some of the practical difficulties of getting there. But for me there were still many problems to be overcome, and - to cut a long story short - I solved most of them by becoming a partner in a small company which we named Island Holidays. We are committed to taking small groups of interested people to the Falklands to enjoy the experience of unspoiled wildlife living - in spite of the conflict - in a largely unspoiled environment.

Our first glimpse of the islands, from the windows of the Royal Air Force Tri-star airliner, gave an almost tropical impression, with light brown plains and hills and beaches of pure white sand, all surrounded by an azure sea.

After landing, which included the formalities of a lecture on the dangers of picking up unidentified objects, we were transported the sixty or so kilometres into the capital town of Stanley, and deposited at our hotel on the waterfront. The view from the bus windows had reinforced some earlier impressions and changed others: the bleached look of the hillsides was caused by the natural colour of white grass

opposite: *This little two-banded plover likes dry, sandy ground with sparse vegetation either near the sea or up on the hills. Its nest is a mere scrape in the ground and both the eggs and the cryptically coloured adults are difficult to spot as they blend in with the surroundings.*

below: *Rock shags build seaweed nests on rocky cliff-faces. In the harbour at Stanley small colonies nest on the old abandoned ships which adorn the waterfront.*

Cordateria pilosa which is dominant over much of the islands. The temperature wasn't quite as tropical as the bright sunlight may have suggested, being held in check by a stiff westerly breeze. Even before we had left the environs of Mount Pleasant airport, we had seen upland geese grazing unconcernedly alongside the runway, and we crossed creeks where small parties of speckled teal were swimming.

The unmistakable shape of a turkey vulture was soaring over the rocky ridge below which the jumbled boulders of the mysterious 'stone runs' flowed in great 'rivers' down the hillsides and out on to almost level ground.

This geological feature is almost unique to the Falkland Islands, and even geologists are not entirely in agreement about how they were formed. Evidently the mountains were much higher in the distant past and these stone runs are the eroded

remains. But how they 'flowed' down to almost level ground is a bit of a mystery. One theory is that they were carried by ice sheets.

We saw a few small birds flitting away from the roadside, but for the moment these had to remain unidentified 'little brown jobs'. But on a hummock by the road a starling-sized bird turned round to reveal a brilliant crimson front which identified it as a long-tailed meadowlark, locally called military starling.

My first impressions were an exciting mixture of scenes that seemed familiar but were so different in detail: I couldn't wait to get a closer look at it all!

We spent the first day getting over the long flight (though with only three hours time difference there was no appreciable jet-lag) and having a look round the town. Some of us found enough to interest us just sitting in front of the Upland Goose Hotel watching the birds in the harbour.

Most obvious were the southern giant petrels: huge, dark brown birds, some with paler heads, and resembling an outsize fulmar, they glide ceaselessly to and fro along the waterfront on wings which can be up to two metres across. Alert for scraps of

Giant petrel.

anything edible, they congregate around the slaughterhouse or sewer outlets and they probably deserve their local name of 'stinker'! Like all the petrels, they are superb exponents of the art of gliding, and awe at their mastery in the air outweighed any doubt about their personal habits.

The remains of several old sailing ships adorn the Stanley waterfront and on some of them rock shags nest along the side decks and in the hawse holes. Their behaviour is quite like that of our common shag, but they have a different diving motion, slipping under the water more in the manner of divers or grebes without any of the upward jump of our birds.

Another noticeable bird of the shores is the flightless steamer duck. It is a large, pugnacious bird like a cross between an eider duck and a goose, and is usually quite unconcerned about human presence. If pushed, it will reluctantly and rather crossly waddle down the beach and take refuge in the sea. The males set up territories which they will defend vigorously against others of their own kind, and fights to the death have occasionally been witnessed. It is a widespread bird all round the Falklands and is called 'logger' by the islanders. A very similar species is the flying steamer duck. It is found more around inland ponds and, as its name suggests, it is capable of flight.

Most of the shore and land birds breeding in the Falklands are resident species: the 'true' seabirds like albatrosses, petrels and penguins move out to sea to largely unknown destinations during the winter. Apart from a few species of northern waders which regularly spend the winter in the islands, the rest of the birds recorded are wind-blown vagrants from South America.

Our second day had been 'earmarked' for a boat trip out to Volunteer Point to see the king penguins, and as it is an open beach, landing is always subject to wind and sea conditions. However conditions seemed promising in the morning and we set off with lunch packs in our bags and hope in our hearts! On the two-hour boat run there are always lots of birds to look at, and soon after we left 'the narrows' of the harbour entrance we were aware of black-browed albatrosses. Gliding ceaselessly on stiffly held wings, they soared and swooped, appearing alternately black or white as they turned their dark backs or their shining white underparts. Their breeding colonies are mainly on headlands or rocky islands off West Falkland.

Suddenly a flock of all-dark shearwaters appeared, only the underwing showing a pale smudge. These were sooty shearwaters and we realised we were passing Kidney Island, a local nature reserve which held large colonies of seabirds, including many thousands of these sooty shearwaters.

Small groups of cormorants with all-white underparts flew past the boat, no doubt heading for some offshore fishing spot. The fact that the white continued up the front of the neck identified them as king cormorants.

Conditions stayed favourable and when we got to the headland of Volunteer Point, the small boat was launched and we were ferried ashore with only the odd wet foot resulting from the landing.

The sea cabbage *Senecio candicans* was in full bloom along the top of the beach and the white-headed clumps of nassauvia, a plant endemic to the Falklands, were dotted among the sand dunes. We happily 'botanised' our way along the shore and then struck inland to where the penguins had established their colony. Nothing had quite prepared us for the sheer presence of king penguins. They stood there, almost a metre tall, regarding our intrusion with no more than mild curiosity. This colony of about 250 pairs is the largest in the Falklands, the king penguin's true home being further south, in islands such as South Georgia and the South Shetlands.

It is easy enough to see why this bird has no need for the power of flight, but found a greater advantage in allowing its wings to become efficient paddles. It has few if any enemies in the open sea (although sea-lions take a few near the shore). In any case, wings which could have lifted that huge body would have been far too cumbersome when diving.

To my way of thinking, penguins are superb examples of evolution fitting out a

overleaf:
Norway is only a couple of hundred kilometres from Shetland, an easy flight for the herons which nest in the trees there. The fiords are generally too deep for wading and Shetland voes offer a winter habitat which hardly ever freezes over, and where small fish can easily be caught on the gently sloping shorelines.

bird to make the best use of its environment - the only potential problem being man.

King penguins were nesting on the bare ground a short walk from our landing beach, and while some still had eggs (which are hatched on top of the feet under a fold of skin on the belly), others already had young, some of whom had developed brown down which made them look like teddy bears!

King penguins are the second largest of all the penguin tribe, only exceeded in size by the emperor penguin which breeds on the sea ice of the cold Antarctic continent. Kings are probably the most handsome of all the penguins: the plumage follows the general pattern of white below and dark above, but the most outstanding features are the golden/orange 'ear-patches' extending to the upper breast.

A single egg is laid, usually from November onwards, and is incubated for about eight weeks. The parents then feed the chick for up to a year. This means that the breeding cycle takes more than a year to complete, with the result that the birds are unable to breed every year.

The weather still held good next day, so we opted for another, shorter, boat trip, this time out to Kidney Island. Landing on the beach presented no problems, though finding a passage through the kelp beds near the shore took some time. We were faced with a daunting barrier of head-high tussac grass with which the island is completely covered. It is little wonder that the early sailors who first saw the Falkland coastline reported 'forests' growing along the shore!

The nutritional value of tussac was perhaps not recognised in the early days and much was destroyed by fire or overgrazing. Now enlightened farmers are fencing off and replanting areas which can be selectively utilised for animal feeding.

The guide had no qualms about the 'forest' (in spite of telling us that sea-lions sometimes hid in the grass to moult!) and set off. Our party followed rather tentatively.

Tussac grass grows in individual clumps, new growth springing up on old, resulting in a maze of tightly spaced 'stools' with narrow passageways between, which are often kept open by penguins and other birds - and the occasional large mammal!

We gained in confidence as we pressed on, until suddenly we broke through on to the cliff-top at the other side of the island. I am sure our guide had this well planned, because we were only a few steps away from a group of rockhopper penguins!

Delightful little birds perhaps 40 cm tall, they have long, pale yellow head-plumes which give them a rather 'punk' appearance. But if you are tempted to laugh, remember they also have a strong beak which can deliver a serious nip. Rockhoppers nearly always nest in colonies up on the tops of cliffs, sometimes 30 metres above the sea, which, on the face of it, seems a daft place for a bird which cannot fly! We humans, however, are not given the power to look into the mind of a penguin and must only accept that this is the best way to ensure survival of the species.

Rockhoppers usually come ashore in the evenings and it is well worth a special trip to watch the performance. Individuals and small parties join together in the open water outside the kelp beds, where they swim up and down as if trying to get the courage to attempt the last lap. Then suddenly one or two break ranks and begin to 'porpoise' shorewards: the rest follow like a school of flying fish!

When they reach the base of the cliff they leap out of the waves, scrabbling for a foothold and not stopping until they are well out of reach of the sea. After a rest and a preen they then put their feet together and hop, hop, hop upwards all the way to the nesting colony on the cliff-top. The reason for this behaviour may be that sea-lions sometimes lie in wait among the kelp near the shore, ready to grab an unwary bird as it makes the transition from the safety of the deep sea to the land.

In some places the path we followed was marked out by deep scratches in the rocks, made by the claws of countless rockhopper penguins who have followed the same traditional route for centuries.

Yet another species of penguin nests on Kidney Island, the Magellanic or 'jackass' penguin. This bird is distinctly different in character from those we had seen so far. They are shy and distrustful, nesting deep inside burrows which they dig out either under the tussac 'stools' or in open turf. The local name comes from the loud braying call which is always at its loudest at four o'clock in the morning, just when you are looking for a bit more sleep after a tiring day.

Turkey vultures are common on Kidney Island and are usually to be seen soaring on two-tone black and translucent wings, peering down at visitors with a calculating look in their beady eye set in a head of bare red skin. Little is to be seen or heard during the day of the thousands of 'night birds' which nest deep in the tussac stools. Only the white-chinned petrel makes an occasional sortie past or drops down in the tussac. A large bird, it comes between sooty shearwater and giant petrel in size, and is called the 'shoemaker' from its repetitive call, said to be like the tapping of a cobbler's hammer.

After two or three days of exploring Stanley and its environs it was time to go to 'camp' (from a Spanish word 'campos' meaning countryside) and our tour of the islands took us to the three or four places equipped to deal with small parties of visitors.

Pebble Island is situated off the north shores of West Falkland, and has a lot to offer the birdwatcher: large colonies of penguins, king cormorants and other cliff- and shore-nesting species including several pairs of the superb red-backed hawk. But more than most places it specialises in wildfowl, because it boasts a number of freshwater lakes and ponds.

It is *the* place for black-necked swans, a superb bird which has its main breeding grounds in the southern parts of Chile and Argentina. It is a large swan with a white body and - as its name suggests - a black head and neck. Its bill is blue/grey with a

Gentoo penguin in the Falklands.

right: *Several kinds of dolphins are seen from time to time in the inshore waters round the Falkland Islands. The easiest to identify is the Commerson's dolphin, because of its 'pied', black and white colouring. It is a friendly little animal, always keen to follow a boat for a 'race' and coming in to quite shallow water at times.*

below: *The most magnificient of all the penguins is the king penguin. The largest colony is at Volunteer Point a few kilometres north of Stanley, where over two hundred birds lay their eggs on the bare ground a few hundred metres from the sea. At about a metre tall they are exceeded in size only by the emperor penguin, which is a vagrant to the Falklands, its breeding grounds being much further south on the Antarctic continent.*

above: *It is always worth looking carefully through the large colonies of rockhopper penguins in case they have been joined by a macaroni penguin. The striking yellow head plumes give the bird a distinctly 'punk' appearance!*

left: *Two kinds of oystercatcher nest in the Falklands, the Magellanic and the blackish. Magellanics look fairly similar to the European oystercatcher. while the one in the photograph is the blackish oystercatcher. As its name suggests, it is brownish/black all over.*

large red knob at the base. Unlike many of the Falkland birds, it is shy and wary, moving out into the middle of the lakes whenever anyone appears. Its nest, in which a clutch of half a dozen eggs is laid, is usually built up of twigs and grass on islets in large ponds or lakes.

For company on the ponds, the swans usually have a selection of ducks such as yellow-billed pintail, Chiloë wigeon, Patagonian crested duck, silver teal and speckled teal. An interesting feature of all these ducks (for which I have no explanation to offer) is that unlike most species of European ducks there is little or no difference between the sexes.

The swans and most of the duck species are not very approachable, usually moving out to the middle of the ponds if people approach too closely. But there is one exception. The white-tufted or Rolland's grebe is one of two species of grebe resident in the islands, and is one of the most engaging birds imaginable. If you approach a pond where these birds are nesting, they will all come swimming up to the bank nearest to you. They will then dive and display and peer at you with their 'redcurrant' eye, as if seeking approval.

The white-tufted grebe is a race endemic to the Falklands while the silvery grebe is also found in Chile and Argentina. It is not quite so confiding as the white-tufted, but is a charming bird nonetheless. Like many grebes, it carries its young on its back while the other parent supplies it with food, but as the plumage of both parents is similar, it is perhaps unwise to make assumptions as to who does what.

On Pebble Island, a great bay called Elephant Bay has as its border a sandy beach no less than seven kilometres in length. This is used as a landing strip for the inter-island air service which, in the absence of roads, is the backbone of the islands' communication system.

The beach is also part of the 'highway' to the eastern end of the island and is a constant source of interest to wildlife enthusiasts. Peale's dolphins often play just beyond the surf, while the sand at low tide is particularly attractive to several species of wading birds.

Both blackish and Magellanic oystercatchers feed on the rocky reefs exposed by the ebb tide, while two-banded plovers and white-rumped sandpipers seek out little crustaceans and marine worms in the sand. The two-banded plover is a resident species, but the white-rumped sandpiper is a non-breeding visitor from as far away as Arctic Canada. This little bird had travelled all the way from its breeding grounds on the Arctic tundra to its wintering quarters in the Falkland Islands!

On the rocky point near the settlement we came across a small flock of birds which had a very familiar look about them: they were whimbrel, that Arctic version of the curlew which breeds on most of the northern islands, including Shetland. We crept close enough to see the features which set them apart from curlew: the smaller size, relatively shorter bill and pattern of light and dark head-stripes.

Several of the nearer birds got up and flew along the shore, revealing another feature which pin-pointed their origins: the lack of a white rump showed them to be of the race *hudsonicus* which breeds in northern Canada. What an incredible migration for a bird to undertake!

In the past, the Falkland sheep farmers looked on birds of prey as their enemies, but more enlightened attitudes are nowadays evident - at least in areas frequented by the few tourists visiting the islands. Peregrine falcons are still common in many suitable areas, generally on sea cliffs or inland crags. This race is distinctly darker than our British bird and can be seen to good advantage on Sea-lion Island, the most southerly inhabited island in the Falklands.

This is also the place to enjoy the most ridiculously tame bird of prey you have ever seen, the striated caracara. Another bird with a very restricted world range, it is confined to Tierra del Fuego and the Falklands. The islanders call it the Johnny rook. If you sit on a cliff edge on Sea-lion Island to enjoy your pack lunch, as likely as not you will be joined by one or more of these amusing birds. They will gladly accept whatever is offered, even taking anything shiny - like a bit of silver paper - from your fingers! But beware, this tameness leads them to be very bold in defence of their nest, and they will laugh a strident 'heh, heh, heh' as they clip you across the ear with a stiffly held wing-tip!

Crested caracara.

Another caracara, the crested, also nests on Sea-lion but is nowhere near as tame and confiding as the Johnny rook. Its local name of 'carancho' is derived from the Spanish.

Sea-lion Island has a tremendous wealth of wildlife within a comparatively small area (the island is less than eight kilometres long by three across) and has all of the five penguin species regularly nesting in the Falklands.

Those we haven't met so far are the macaroni penguin and the gentoo. Macaronis occur only in small numbers, and are always found nesting in a colony of the fairly similar but less gaudy rockhopper. They are marginally larger and instead of the pale yellow head-plumes are adorned with bright golden-yellow plumes which meet over the forehead. They are similar in habits to the rockhoppers.

overleaf, left:
One of the rarest gulls in the world is the dolphin gull. It is found only in Patagonia and the Falklands. It has striking red feet and bill, while instead of the usual white of most gull species, the head, neck and underparts are pearly grey in colour. Contrasting with the black back and wings, this makes it a very handsome gull.

The gentoo is a large penguin, standing over sixty centimetres tall and is more like the king penguin in its habits, preferring to come ashore on sandy beaches and establish 'rookeries' up on nearby hillsides. It lays two eggs in a scrappy nest made of twigs and grass, and habitually changes to a new colony site each year. Like all penguins gentoos have tremendous swimmers and divers, and when preparing to come ashore they frequently 'porpoise' along in groups more like fish than birds. However, agile and fast as they are, they are sometimes outwitted by sea-lions who lie near the breaking surf off the beaches and come dashing ashore to grab a bird in the 'danger zone' of the shallow water.

above: *The smallest of the Falkland gulls is the brown-hooded gull. It is closely related to the European black-headed gull, but differs in wing pattern and in having a more positive pink flush to its underparts during the breeding season.*

It was tempting to try and do too much on one short visit to the Falklands. The summer breeding season extends between November and February, so we would have to come back again earlier in the season to have a look at some of the other birds, such as the smaller land birds, which tend to present more problems to the photographer.

In any case, the Shetland spring would soon be upon us - and I wouldn't want to miss it.

3 SHETLAND SPRING

'Spring has sprung, the grass has riz,
I wonder where them birdies is!'

When I left the Falkland Islands there were signs that summer there was drawing to a close. Sea-birds were beginning to leave the shores and there were more seeding heads than flowers in bloom. In Britain the opposite was the case, and on the way home I noticed daffodils in bloom and even cherry blossom in sheltered gardens in England. But, apart from a few foolhardy daisies confused by a mild winter, there was little in Shetland to indicate that spring was - officially - only a few weeks away.

Some birds were already on the move, however. Since early February oyster-catchers had been arriving back from spending the winter around the big estuaries of mainland Britain and by the end of March were well distributed in coastal areas. They are no longer confined to the immediate shorelines and the traditional food of limpets and other shellfish, but are more inclined to forage in fields and parkland in company with curlews and starlings. There seems to be no satisfactory explanation for this change in habits, which began about thirty years ago. It was noted in the Faroes (where the oystercatcher is the national bird), in Scotland, where the birds began to penetrate inland up the river valleys, and in Shetland, where they forsook the shingle beaches and moved to fields and even up on the heather hills.

The local radio had reported that someone had heard a skylark singing, and that in Lerwick a blackbird was already on its first clutch of catfood. Poor old blackbirds, they never seem to learn! So often they build nests inside sheds and outbuildings which are the natural homes for the local 'moggies'.

A few early lapwings were on territory, twisting and turning in frantic display, and little doubt the local crows had already noted the fact for future reference.

The months of March and April see the beginning of that great annual movement of birds towards northern breeding grounds. Although winter is still firmly in control in the far northern regions of the Arctic, birds are already preparing for the coming season by moulting into fresh breeding plumage. Many of those which have wintered in the coastal seas or along the shores of Britain gather in the northern islands to complete the moult before attempting the long flight.

Great northern divers, having spent the winter singly in many of the Shetland voes, gather in parties and are joined by birds from further south. They congregate in favoured places such as Quendale Bay, Ronas Voe and north of Hascosay, as they have done for generations, and here they complete their moult into their smart summer dress, to replace the drab dark grey and white. Their head turns glossy green with a double 'necklace' of white stripes on the neck, and the back develops a startling 'chequerboard' of black and white.

When they are ready to be seen on their home territory - which may be northern Scandinavia or Iceland - they disappear, hopefully to come back with their offspring in the autumn.

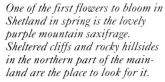

Common winter visitors to Shetland, turnstones tend to stay on the coasts where they can be seen foraging along the shores, flicking over small stones in search of insects and crustaceans.

One of the first flowers to bloom in Shetland in spring is the lovely purple mountain saxifrage. Sheltered cliffs and rocky hillsides in the northern part of the mainland are the place to look for it.

Most of the red-throated divers which appear in the inshore voes at this time will be local breeders, and territories and relationships will be sorted out with much caterwauling and chasing before the successful pair set up home on some peaty pool. There they will remain for most of April, at least one of the pair on guard at all times on the loch in order to ward off any attempted 'take-over', perhaps by young pairs who haven't been able to locate a suitable breeding site. All the while, the eggs are developing ready for laying by the lochside in May.

Long-tailed ducks also prepare to give up their marine existence for their summer home on the tundra pools of Iceland or northern Europe. Some will 'get the taste' of fresh water by moulting on freshwater lochs in Shetland, raising hopes yet again that this attractive duck will one day stay on to nest in Shetland.

Out on the fields, the flocks of golden plover begin to show an increasing number of black-fronted birds as they moult, and the extent of these markings suggest they are of more northerly origin. The fact that they are still here when our local birds are already displaying over their territories reinforces this, because the Arctic spring is still a couple of months away.

It has to be admitted that Shetland is not the most suitable place for wintering waders. It lacks the extensive mud-flats rich in marine invertebrates which attract these birds in their thousands to places like Morecambe Bay or the Washes of England. Only a few places, like the Pool of Virkie at the south end of Shetland, attract waders for a time on migration, and most of them move on to richer pastures for the winter.

But the rocky shore specialists are better catered for and turnstones and purple sandpipers are common winter residents. In April many of the turnstones are starting to show the handsome rich chestnut back markings and cryptic head pattern of their breeding plumage. No doubt some will stay on to summer in Shetland and encourage us to hope that some day it too may be found nesting.

Purple sandpipers are the most self-effacing of birds. We used to call them 'ebb-sleepers' because they were usually found resting on the rocks at high tide in small groups, each bird apparently asleep with its beak tucked under its scapulars.

Most of the small passerines which favour an Arctic summer home, where they can take advantage of the prolific insect life, pass through Shetland on their way to a winter habitat which suits their food preferences. But there are a few exceptions in the seed-eating species like finches and buntings. In a mild winter where snow cover is not prolonged, chaffinch and brambling from the Scandinavian forests will stay on to forage round the crofts. Sometimes they will be joined by 'mealy' redpolls - so called because of their paler plumage - from farther north, or even the more exotic Arctic redpoll with its beautiful 'frosted' plumage.

Also from the Arctic and mountainous regions are the snow buntings, and these are a characteristic feature of the Shetland winter, as lively flocks of 'snaafowls' forage on the stubble. (Their name means 'snow-birds' in Shetlandic.) In March or April the flocks take on an even whiter appearance as the males moult into 'whiter than white' plumage with only a black mantle.

Out at sea, apart from the lengthening days, only changes in bird life suggest that spring has arrived.

The composition of the flocks of birds following the fishing-boats will be changing. Glaucous gulls and any other northern stragglers such as Iceland and

Fair Isle Bird Observatory was established in some disused navy huts just after the last war by the late George Waterston. A fine new building can now cater for the needs of well over twenty birdwatchers, scientists or other visitors.

Purple sandpipers breed on the tundra in Iceland and northern Scandinavia, resorting to coastal areas farther south in the winter-time. Self-effacing birds, they are easily overlooked as they sit quietly among the rocks, their unremarkable plumage merging with their surroundings.

Gannets in a greeting display.

perhaps ivory gulls will drift off towards their Arctic breeding-grounds. They will be replaced by lesser black-backed gulls, the only Shetland breeding gull which entirely deserts the islands in winter.

More gannets will be arriving daily from winter quarters, which may be as far south as the coastal waters of West Africa and with them will come the great skuas to harry them for food.

Later in April Arctic skuas will arrive as the kittiwake population builds up near the shores, back from their pelagic winter wanderings, and timing their return to coincide with the arrival of shoals of immature fish which swarm in the surface layers of the sea.

The auk tribe (guillemots, razorbills and puffins), which spend the winter scattered widely over the ocean, will also be heading inshore towards their breeding cliffs. Some guillemots and razorbills will have stayed in inshore waters during the winter, and will even roost on breeding ledges early in the year, but puffins will rarely be seen inshore until late April.

The other member of the auks to breed in Shetland, the black guillemot, stays inshore all year, and will now have completed its moult from mottled grey and white to the smart satin black with white wing-patches. It will be making early morning visits to the boulder beaches and broken cliffs where it will later lay its two large spotted eggs well out of sight in some crevice.

The numbers of little auks which winter in the tidal streams round the islands, and the occasional Brünnich's guillemot which turns up, are of northern origin, the Brünnich's breeding no nearer than Iceland or the north tip of Norway, and the little auks from the area of Spitsbergen.

The auk tribe are sea-birds in the true sense, in that they do not need the land at all outside the nesting season. Even our local guillemot or tystie rarely comes on land except to nest.

Auks have evolved into rather specialised birds; they have become adapted to finding and catching their food beneath the sea surface to the extent that they are unable to do things any other way. This is fine so long as that food is readily available, but it means that the birds are rather vulnerable should there be any changes in circumstances.

Some changes may be natural, such as those in the flow and direction of ocean currents, which can affect the distribution of the small pelagic fish or fish fry on which the birds depend. Temperature changes also can influence the depth at which the fish swim.

Man's activities can affect sea-birds in many ways: pollution of the sea, either by chemical effluents dispersed in the water column which may poison their food, or surface pollution, for example, by oil spillage, can be the direct cause of death to birds which have no option but to use the sea surface. Predation by man on the bigger fish should, in theory, leave more small fish for the birds, but sadly, 'industrial' fishing for even the smallest and immature fish is a fact of life which has serious implications for the very existence of our sea-bird communities should it be allowed to go on unchecked.

While many of the changes which take place in the bird world in spring pass unremarked - if not unnoticed - the first arrivals of our summer migrants always excite comment. Who could fail to notice the resplendent little cock wheatears by the roadside? Singing constantly from a prominent post or in flight, they show off their beautiful spring black, white, grey and buff spring plumage in the hope it will prove irresistible to the first passing female.

Also song-flighting up on the moors, the less showy meadow pipit returns during April from spending the winter in places where the weather is less severe, but its cousin the rock pipit is made of sterner stuff and spends the winter in Shetland, sharing the shoreline habitat with the Shetland wren.

Along with the returning small birds comes the merlin, their only serious predator. *Little auks.* The merlin establishes its territory up in the heather-covered hill areas, and searches out suitable hooded crows' nests from the year before which it will appropriate for its own brood. It does seem unfair that a wheatear or pipit, having survived all the dangers of migration, should arrive home to find a merlin has set up house in its territory!

So, spring is the time of great activity in the bird world, and few events are more

Eiders have traditional wintering places in the sheltered 'sounds' between the islands. Here they gather in flocks to feed on molluscs and crustaceans from the sandy sea-bed, coming ashore to rest and preen on nearby beaches such as here at Lingey, an island between Yell and Unst.

exciting to birdwatchers in Shetland than the spring passage of migrants. Anxiously we watch the skies for change and listen to the weather forecasts; words like 'high pressure areas', 'occlusions', 'fronts' and 'anti-cyclones' intersperse the conversation when birdwatchers foregather. For everything depends on the weather; most birds - even tiny scraps like goldcrests - can make the 'North Sea hop' in one go, and would no doubt would prefer to give Shetland a miss. After all, there is not much in the way of food available in the early spring for those birds dependent on insects.

But Shetland enjoys - or should it be suffers from - a mild, oceanic type of climate, typified by depressions moving east from the Atlantic Ocean. If these depressions

Spotted flycatchers are seen fairly frequently on migration in Shetland, though with our windy climate, the flying insects on which they feed are not always easy to find.

(or low pressure areas) are tracking in towards Ireland rather than taking a more northerly route, then the circulation of wind flowing clockwise (as it must) round the depression means that south-easterly winds will be blowing over Shetland from the North Sea and pushing any birds unfortunate enough to be flying to (or from) Scandinavia at the time in a westerly direction.

The circulation of air round a depression usually has 'fronts' or areas of rain associated with it, and when birds, which navigate by being able to see the night sky, meet with a barrier of rain and bad visibility then there is nothing for it but to drop down to the nearest land and wait until conditions improve. This is why, after a night of south-easterly winds and rain in spring or in autumn, you can find the islands littered with small birds of many species, all desperately trying to find some food which can replenish the energy reserves sufficiently to enable them to continue on their way as soon as weather allows.

While Shetland has probably always been a sort of filling-station for birds on migration, it is too big an area for even the most energetic birdwatcher to cover, and thousands of birds arrive and depart unseen. And while there a number of local 'hot-

Among the many small migrant birds which visit the northern islands in spring on their way to Scandinavia, willow warblers are probably the most numerous. This is a common breeding bird in all the forested areas of Scandinavia, extending even beyond the Arctic Circle. It is also found in suitable areas of Britain.

Cock wheatear.

spots' such as Out Skerries, the islands of Fetlar and Unst, the southern part of the mainland and almost any plantations of trees, there is only one name that every migrant watcher and twitcher knows - Fair Isle.

Fair Isle is a cliff-bound island of only about five hundred hectares in extent and lies midway between Orkney and Shetland. A human population of about sixty people make their living from crofting, knitting and a small amount of lobster-fishing. The distinctive Fair Isle knitting patterns are known (and copied) the world over.

The seas surrounding the island are notoriously rough, due to the strong tidal currents which sweep past the islands; the worst is the Sumburgh Roost which, with an adverse wind, can cause huge 'overfalls'. It is little wonder that Fair Isle has an unenviable history of shipwrecks. Until quite recently the only way to get to Fair Isle was by boat from Shetland, and a succession of island-based craft have carried the name of 'Good Shepherd'. To many hundreds of birdwatchers the name conjures up either the anticipation or satisfaction of excellent birding, or memories of the abject miseries of seasickness on the three-hour crossing.

Nowadays a flight of fifteen minutes in an 'Islander' aircraft makes life a lot easier for sufferers from *mal-de-mer* - visitors and islanders alike - although all heavy supplies still come in by sea.

Fair Isle first came into prominence as a bird migration station as long ago as 1912, following publication of a book by William Eagle-Clarke, keeper of the natural history department of the Royal Scottish Museum. He spent some weeks on the island in 1905 and, with the help of an islander, George Stout, kept up regular observations, including a complete diary of the year 1908.

Other well-known ornithologists followed, including such notable personages as the then Duchess of Bedford, but it was not until 1948 that a 'proper' bird observatory was established by the late Dr George Waterston. He had been visiting the island since 1935 and during his internment as a prisoner of war he worked up plans to establish an observatory on the island after the war.

Although Fair Isle is officially part of Shetland, and I had been a keen birdwatcher since I was a boy, I had never had the opportunity to visit the island until I had started to work for the Royal Society for the Protection of Birds.

The major restriction had, of course, been the war, following which I entered an apprenticeship as a baker. My wages of twenty-five shillings (£1.25) a week did not permit birdwatching trips far afield and, although I was fairly keen and competent, I was bounded by pretty narrow horizons! But when I joined the RSPB in 1964 as their Shetland representative, I began the process of getting to know the islands better, and this included making the first of many visits to Fair Isles. Only then did I begin to see what I had been missing.

In April 1964 I arranged with Roy Dennis, who had recently been appointed as warden of the bird observatory, to visit the island for a week to get the experience and expertise required before I could apply for a permit to catch and ring birds. Watching birds is only the enjoyable tip of the study of ornithology: protection, population studies, learning about the lives of individual birds, including the study of migration, are just a few of the many other facets. Ringing (or banding, as it is termed in America) is a most useful tool for many of these studies. So, as a practising ornithologist, I wished to obtain the necessary skills.

Although the week was reckoned to be a quiet one by Fair Isle standards, I not only added eight 'new' birds to my life list, but made a number of friends who remain friends to this day.

At that time the observatory was housed in some rather dilapidated wooden huts which had seen service with the Royal Navy during the war, and these were later replaced by a fine purpose-built building which offered much better accommodation and laboratory facilities. But the memories of the old observatory linger still. Of the feeling of expectancy if the wind was in the right direction. Of doing the rounds of the 'Heligoland' traps before breakfast in the morning to see whether the night had brought any ' new' birds.

These traps are large constructions of poles and wire netting which were first devised on the island of Heligoland, off the German coast in the North Sea. They are strategically erected in places favoured by migrant birds, such as over stone walls or steep-sided streams, and are often planted with trees and bushes in order to encourage birds into the 'tunnel' which ends in a glass-fronted catching box.

Thanks to this device many thousands of birds have been caught, weighed, measured and then had a lightweight metal ring clamped round one leg before being released in the hope that, when it is next caught (or perhaps found dead), the number stamped on the ring will be seen and reported. In this way information is gradually built up, helping to paint a picture of the lives and lifestyles of the birds which appear so dramatically in the islands.

The birds caught in the traps on Fair Isle will be mainly the smaller passerines such as warblers, chats and the like, which tend to seek out any cover available. Some of the huge flocks of Scandinavian thrushes (fieldfare, redwing, and song-thrush mainly) which pass through in spring and autumn, will enter the traps but the majority will stay out on the hillsides.

There are two lighthouses on Fair Isle, and if a night of muggy sea-mist coincided

It is a sad fact that many small land birds must perish each year through becoming exhausted during long sea crossings - especially in adverse weather. This skylark landed on my boat one day in thick fog, and sat on the deck until I got within sight of land, when it flew off towards the shore.

with a passage of thrushes, thousands of birds might be attracted and confused by the lights. If this happened the lighthouse-keeper would tell the warden, who would muster as many 'hands' as were available, and go up to the headlands where the lighthouses stood.

Hundreds of birds might be circling the lighthouse in the misty darkness, illuminated briefly as the beam swung round in a circle. Every now and again a thrush would land on the ground exhausted, to be netted and put in with others in a cardboard box. In the darkness of the box they would sit quietly and in the morning would be ringed and released.

The lighthouse-keeper's wife would kindly allow us to store the boxes of birds in her bathroom until they were ready to be moved. I vividly remember the occasion when a box had not been properly secured - when poor Katy opened the bathroom door she was greeted by a scene which must have been reminiscent of the Hitchcock film *The Birds* with thrushes and feathers flying everywhere!

I also well remember the shame I felt when, having caught a pipit which was bearing a foreign ring, I accidentally let the bird escape from my hand before anyone had a chance to check the ring number. Needless to say, it was never seen again.

The work of the observatory is not confined to migrant birds, and there are on-going studies on the many thousands of sea-birds which nest in the cliffs.

opposite: Shetland is practically treeless except for one or two of the sheltered limestone valleys, where plantations of trees of various species flourish. In the valley of Weisdale, a farm called Kergord has the best plantations in Shetland. They were established about 150 years ago, and have attracted a few species of birds such as rooks, wood pigeons and occasional small birds to breed. They are also attractive to migrant birds such as this golden oriole, which although so conspicuous out in the fields is not at all easy to see in the thick vegetation.

Over 340 species of birds have been recorded on Fair Isle and this includes a number of 'firsts' for Britain, such as the eastern Siberian Pallas's reed bunting, and the east European Cretzschmar's bunting. Transatlantic birds such as the Tennessee warbler and Blackburnian warbler have also turned up in Fair Isle, amazing journeys for small birds, and especially so if they depend on insects for food, as most warblers do. Only a small proportion are caught and ringed, of course, and throughout the migration season the wardens and any visitors patrol the island, checking all the likely spots, and talking to the islanders, many of whom are interested and knowledgeable about their birds.

By evening, almost every bird on the island will have been 'logged' in someone's note book, and, after supper, 'doing the log' is one of the highlights of the day as everyone recounts - and relives - the day's happenings. Bluethroats in the cabbage patches, aquatic warblers in the drainage ditches, harlequin duck in the harbour and snowy owl on the hill. It has all happened in the past and may well happen again - and again - in the future.

Whimbrel.

4 LAPPLAND - THE HOME OF THE NORTHERN BIRDS

It was a good conference: the venue was familiar and comfortable, the speakers were good and the general theme of 'northern birds' had produced interesting lectures. Of equal importance, the social side was satisfactory. Many old friends had been greeted and new friends made. Late on the Saturday evening, in the glow which follows a good dinner and good wines, four of us, all old acquaintances, were sitting at a table in the lounge talking - inevitably - about birds, and the conversation got round to places we would like to visit.

My contribution was on the lines that having seen so many birds passing through Shetland on migration, I would love to follow them to their breeding-grounds in northern Scandinavia. We all agreed that, none of us having been there, Lappland had an aura of romantic mystery about it, but wasn't it a difficult and expensive place to get to?

After glasses had been refilled one of us - Tony, I think - said, 'Why do we just talk about it? Why don't we do it?' and we all agreed rather tentatively that it might be a good idea.

Well, unlike many of the promises that are made over the clinking of glasses and in the glow of a few drinks, and despite the fact that Pam and Tony lived near Thurso in the north of Scotland, Wendy was working in Bristol and I lived in Shetland, we got in touch later and laid firm plans for a trip to Lappland.

We decided that we would like to spend much of our available time in the far north, beyond the Arctic Circle so, taking turns at driving and stopping only for fuel and occasional snacks, we thrashed on up the 'spine' of Norway through spectacular mountain scenery to Trondheim. Much of the country was wooded and the birds were not too obvious. The continental form of our pied wagtail, the white wagtail, was common along the roads, often fly-catching on the tarmac. This wagtail is the one most commonly seen in Shetland on migration, and is distinguished from the race breeding in southern parts of Britain by having a grey rather than a black back.

The occasional thrush flew across in front of the car; once we had a glimpse of a woodpecker of some kind, and early one morning a badger trotted across the road.

But wherever we stopped, the woods were full of birdsong. I didn't recognise much of it because birds passing through Shetland on migration are not on territory and therefore have little inclination to advertise their presence by singing.

A short distance south of Trondheim we turned off down a side road to find a quiet spot for lunch, and in a grove of trees we saw redwing, fieldfare and chaffinch feeding young while siskin, blackcap, chiffchaff and willow warbler were singing all around us. All these species are common migrants which appear in Shetland every year, and I couldn't help wondering if any of those we were hearing and seeing may have been feeding in the bushes in my garden a short time before. . .

From Trondheim we went over the mountain ridge and the border into Sweden. The road ran through seemingly interminable pine forests with little to encourage

A typical finch of the Scandinavian woods is the brambling. Its nest is normally placed fairly high up in the trees which makes photography difficult. On this occasion the mountainside was steep and although the nest was over ten metres above the ground, it was on a level with the road. I took the photograph from the bus window!

us to stop and explore, and we covered over 1300 kilometres in thirty hours. As we neared the Arctic Circle, the country opened up more, with extensive marshes dotted with willow and birch trees. We called a halt near Kitanga.

We had come armed with maps and information from birding friends, and this spot was marked with a cross indicating it was a good place for waders. It may have been, but now it was inhabited by millions of hungry mosquitoes! We floundered around for an hour or so, seeing a few wood sandpipers and dusky redshanks (who invariably saw us first).

Known in Shetland only as passage migrants, these two waders are the most obvious birds of these Scandinavian marshes: the wood sandpiper is the smaller of the two - and the noisier!

The dusky (or spotted) redshank is a most unusual-looking wader. About the same size as our familiar British redshank, in breeding plumage it is almost black all over with some paler spotting on the back. It is equally all-seeing and noisy in defence of its nest.

But the 'mozzies' finally won the day and we retreated back to the safety of the 'bus' to lick our wounds and to hunt out our supplies of insect repellent! Shetland has no biting insects apart from a few midges in late summer, and I hadn't realised just how much of a problem these Arctic mosquitoes could be. The Swedish marshes provide ideal breeding-grounds and the lack of wind in summer ideal flying conditions for mosquitoes; at times they were so bad that we were reluctant to get out to explore these excellent marshy habitats fully. It was probably for this reason that we missed some of the more esoteric waders like broad-billed sandpiper and jack snipe which are known to nest in this area.

We crossed the Arctic Circle without ceremony, the only indication a large noticeboard by the roadside and a row of white-painted boulders disappearing into the trees at either side. The weather was warm and humid and it was difficult to believe that we were now officially in the Arctic. But notices warning of reindeer and even of moose (elk) crossing-places kept us in reality, and soon the country began to open out, forests giving way to scrubby birch and willows with rolling hills and quiet lakes in the valleys.

We spotted our first reindeer lying down in a hollow by the roadside some distance ahead and, as I had a telephoto lens on the camera, the others encouraged me to have a go at stalking it. So I wormed my way along the roadside ditch, getting torn and scratched by thorns in the process, until I judged I was opposite to where the animal lay, peaceably chewing the cud. Ever so slowly I raised my head and camera and there it was. The beast didn't appear to have seen me and I took several photographs. Then, mindful of my companions, I crawled back the way I had come, getting muddier and acquiring even more scratches.

My pleasure at the success of the operation turned a bit sour when the others calmly walked up the road and photographed the animal with standard lenses - and it didn't even bother getting up.

However, we spotted its calf frisking among the trees and it was more elusive. It was only by using the telephoto lens that I was able to take its picture - and it was much prettier than its mother anyway.

Although we had been in the land of constant daylight for several days, the sun had been hidden for much of the time by high cloud. But as we travelled down a lovely wooded valley towards the north coast at Alta, the sun appeared below the clouds near midnight and we stopped to take our first pictures of the midnight sun. We pitched camp that night to the accompaniment of the song of a cock snow bunting in the rocks nearby.

From Alta, which is a small fishing village, our chosen route took us over the high plateau towards Varanger Fiord. We ran into some bad weather on the way, with heavy rain followed by thick fog, which was frustrating because we were at times up near the permanent snowline, and had occasional glimpses of birds like rough-legged buzzard, with Lappland bunting and red-throated pipits by the roadside.

Varanger Fiord is quite unlike the spectacular steep-sided fiords of western Norway. It is more a wide bay with mostly low foreshores, opening out to the north-east into the Barents Sea. The variety of shores make it particularly good for birds such as waders and sea duck, and its situation 'next door' to Siberia makes seeing even more exciting birds a possibility.

A typical 'roadside' bird in Scandinavia is the white wagtail. It often feeds by catching insects near the road. It is a race of the familiar British pied wagtail, only differing in having a grey rather than a black back.

Although quite rare in Britain except as a migrant, the wood sandpiper is common in the marshes of northern Scandinavia. It uses willow and birch trees as a look-out post and is extremely watchful and 'all-seeing'.

At Nesseby we found a tiny peninsula with cliffs just high enough for a colony of kittiwakes, which were all feeding large young. As usual, they were nesting on a precipitous - though in this case well-vegetated - cliff-face. The successful birds had two young which were feathered well enough to show the black bar along the grey wings which distinguishes immature kittiwakes.

On top of the headland there was a boggy area covered in dwarf cornel with its white flowers, and a number of small pools. On these pools, red-necked phalarope were feeding in numbers, and in one group of over seventy was a solitary grey phalarope, probably a visitor from the far north. The nearest known breeding-place is Bear Island, or perhaps Novaya Zemyla, the large island to the north of Siberia.

A few tiny waders attracted our attention feeding round the edges of the pools, and a close look identified them as stints, both little stint and Temminck's stint. The stints are the smallest of the waders, and these two species have fairly similar plumages of streaky brown with paler underparts. But the Temminck's stint has a greyer, more uniform look and its legs are dull yellow, whereas those of the little stint are black.

Steller's Eider duck.

I had seen these birds before in Shetland, but only in winter plumage on migration, and here they were, obviously on their home territory. As we watched, some of them took flight and went into their circling display, calling all the time. The longer, undulating trilling of the little stint was then the easiest way of telling the two species apart.

Other birds we saw around Nesseby included dunlin, familiar enough to me as a breeding wader of the Shetland hills. Ruff were displaying their fantasy plumes to their more soberly dressed wives. In winter plumage (as we mostly see them in Shetland) they are brown waders with a 'scaly' appearance, a little larger than redshank. But in summer the male ruff is an amazing-looking bird with a variously coloured 'ruff' of long feathers round its neck which it can fan out in nuptial display. The ruff can be almost any shade of cream or red to black, and includes ear-tufts often of a different colour.

Scanning the area with our glasses, we found a party of eider duck and were excited to see that the flock not only contained common and king eider, but a number of Steller's eider, a 'new' bird for all of us, which breeds along the Siberian coast and into Alaska. Females of the three species have sombre plumage of dark brown, and it needs a practised eye to tell female king eider from common eider. But Steller's eider is distinctly smaller and usually shows white wing-bars.

Males are easy to tell apart when in full breeding dress: the familiar common eider with its black and white body and a patch of sea green on its nape; the unmistakable king eider with its large orange 'knob' on the forehead; and the smaller Steller's eider with chestnut underparts. Unfortunately for birdwatchers, the three species are most likely to be seen together in summer when the males will probably be moulting into their so-called 'eclipse' plumage.

Most duck species undergo a double moult. They lose their often gaudy plumage in early summer after nesting is complete, exchanging it for a drab and less conspicuous dress for the summer and autumn. During this time, the flight feathers are all replaced simultaneously, making the bird flightless for a while. Often the males moult in flocks separately from the females, and only after the second moult in autumn do they regain their finery and again join up with their wives.

The main road which follows the north shores of Varanger Fiord ends just past the small town of Vardø, but a rough track continues on round the headland. It looked enticing and we decided to follow it as far as we could. It led to an abandoned fishing hamlet called Hamningberg, where we camped for the night in a grassy field studded with interesting saxifrages and other flowers.

It was difficult to believe we were over four hundred kilometres north of the Arctic Circle. The sea was calm, the sky was blue and with the sun beating on the tent it was almost too warm to zip up my sleeping-bag. We were camped out on a headland and could see groups of birds flying past. Most of them had the familiar 'jizz' of guillemots but were too far out for us to tell if they were common guillemots or the Arctic species, Brünnich's guillemots. ('Jizz' is a term coined by experienced birdwatchers to explain how a distant or fleeting glimpse of a bird can produce a positive identification without your being able to say exactly why.)

In with the guillemots were small parties of gannets, and we wondered if there was a breeding colony this far north, as most gannet colonies are on sub-Arctic islands.

All of the birds appeared to be heading towards a high headland far across on the other side of the bay and, according to our map, this headland was called Fuglafjell - 'bird mountain'. It appeared to have a road running to within a few kilometres. We decided there and then that would be our next target.

While on 'seawatch', we saw a couple of large divers near the shore. To our delight these turned out to be white-billed divers, another species which breeds farther east along the Siberian coast. The birds had a habit of dipping their beaks in the water and then shaking their heads so that the ivory-coloured beaks flashed in the sun.

For several kilometres the track to Hamningberg follows the shoreline, in places along beaches covered in driftwood logs. We disturbed a huge sea-eagle eating something on the shore, and it flapped heavily away round the headland. There were flocks of moulting eiders and quite a lot of goosanders in the bays, as well as a number of turnstones in their smart 'tortoiseshell' breeding plumage along the shores.

Back at the head of Varanger Fiord, we turned off north on what we hoped was the road to Fuglafjell and got as far as the fishing village of Syltefiord. We found that the walk to Fuglafjell was farther (and much rougher) than we had anticipated, so we

North beyond the treeline in Scandinavia is the home of the Lappland bunting. It defends and advertises its territory by singing in flight like a skylark, though neither the song nor the flight is as sustained as that bird's. The Lappland bunting is seen on migration in Britain, mainly in the eastern coastal areas.

persuaded a fisherman to take us to the bird cliffs in his boat. It was late at night and although the sun was still above the horizon, low cloud made photography from the boat impossible. Nevertheless it was a rewarding trip: this is the most northerly gannet colony in the world, and is also the home of five different species of auks. We saw common guillemot, Brünnich's guillemot, razorbill, black guillemot and puffin: it only needed little auk to complete all the auks on the European list!

On the low ground nearby where the vegetation cover was extensive, birds were also plentiful. There were red-throated pipits, a bird but rarely seen in Britain while on migration, and which I first identified on Out Skerries. They look a bit like our familiar meadow pipit apart from the chestnut colour of the throat. They were feeding young, but were rather shy about having their photograph taken.

The bluethroat has been a favourite bird of mine ever since the day, many years ago when I was a small boy, that this bird with the beautiful blue gorget flew out of our cabbage patch and perched on the stone wall. I had never before seen such a beautiful bird! In its nesting ground in Scandinavia it appears reluctant to show off its finery, preferring to stay in the depths of the vegetation.

The ruff breeds far north along the shore of Varanger Fiord in Norway. Males are real dandies: they grow a variously coloured neck 'ruff' and gather in groups or 'leks' where they prance around and display to each other while the smaller and unadorned females stand around and watch.

When the breeding season is over, the males lose their fancy 'capes' and become more like the females, though they are always noticeably larger. The scaly pattern on the back is a good identification feature.

Snow buntings, their throats bulging with food for hungry nestlings, paid little attention to us, and Lappland buntings were singing from the top of boulders, the males with striking head patterns in their summer plumage. The two bunting species are very different in appearance. Snow bunting males are unmistakable in their all-white plumage with black backs. The females are more muted in brown and white. Male Lappland buntings have streaked brown backs with striking black, white and chestnut heads. Females look a bit like our female reed buntings, having a streaked appearance all over.

Two birds swooping through the air at tremendous speed caught our eye, and we watched spellbound as a pair of long-tailed skuas gave a tremendous display of aerobatics before settling on the tundra not far away. We found the nest with two brown spotted eggs, and the pair hovered overhead as we took a quick look, giving me a chance to photograph them against the blue Arctic sky.

But time was pressing on and we were a long way from home. We had a quick look at the little town of Berlevåg, where we joined a crowd of youngsters around a hot-dog stall at two o'clock in the morning. 'When do you sleep?' I asked a blond-haired little boy. 'In the winter,' he replied with a cheeky grin.

We decided to do one last detour before heading south and remembering advice we had been given, we headed past Kirkenes towards the Pasvik Elv, the valley and river which form the border between Norway and Russia. Although we saw one or two birds such as pine grosbeak, waxwing and bean goose which were 'new' for the trip, we found the valley a depressing place. The weather turned sour with thunderstorms and heavy rain. The battery on the 'bus' showed signs of dying and border guards were suspicious - I suppose my long telephoto lens did look a bit like an anti-tank gun!

Worst of all, the mosquitoes returned in force and succeeded in penetrating our defences in spite of Djungel Olja, a recommended Swedish preparation, and 'mosquito coils' which burnt like joss sticks with a smell almost as unpleasant as the bite of the insects.

We made camp that night in a clearing in the woods, and I put up my tent in what appeared to be a large sandpit, in the vague hope that perhaps the mozzies might not like it. I suppose I should have noticed that the sand was all trampled but I wasn't to know that the sandpit was the personal stamping ground of a large bull reindeer. I was awakened sometime in the small hours with a snorting and snuffling and a large shadow on my tent. Remembering that a couple of kilometres back we had seen a huge moose lumbering across the road, I peered fearfully through a slit in my tent to see this massive reindeer with bloodshot eyes and antlers that appeared to be three metres across. He was pawing the sand and throwing it about with his antlers. I was convinced he was about to do the same to me, when he suddenly appeared to notice the tent for the first time, shied away and crashed off into the trees. It was a long time before I fell asleep that night!

It was homeward bound after that and we motored south through Finland's seemingly endless pine forests, past huge lakes with unpronounceable names and rivers with great rafts of pine logs en-route for the sawmills. We crossed over the river into Sweden near the Baltic coast at Haparanda (and suffered the embarrassment of having to be push started to get off the ferry) and drove on to Lulea where we called a halt because I had promised to say hello to a friend of a friend who lived there.

Valdemar was extremely helpful and took the next day off work to show us some of the local birds. We arranged to meet outside his local church, and first of all he took us to a garage where he negotiated a good price for a new car battery! Then we went to a lake with wooded and marshy shores where we saw several 'new' birds: a crane flew past, looking like a grey heron except that it carried its neck outstretched in flight instead of 'folded back'. A little gull was hawking insects over the marsh, its characteristic dark underwings showing as it banked. If it was a breeding bird it would be on the northern edge of its range.

An unusual call led us to the reeds by the lake, and it turned out to be an ortolan

Arctic terns.

bunting, quite distinctive with its buff chest and olive-green head. A summer breeding visitor to most of eastern Europe, it is only a vagrant to Britain. I had first seen it on Out Skerries during spring migration.

After we left the lake, our friend drove us inland to a forested area where, he assured us we had a good chance of seeing a great grey owl. The great grey is one of the largest of the forest owls of Scandinavia, larger even than the snowy owl of the Arctic tundra, and one species we had little hope of finding unaided.

After walking for some time through the wood Valdemar put his finger to his lips and motioned us to be quiet. Pointing upwards he indicated a large nest high in a pine tree and told us that it was the nest of a buzzard which had been taken over by a great grey owl. As the young owls had fledged, he said that we might expect to find them anywhere in the area, and that the best idea was for us to fan out and scan the branches. So we moved outwards in different directions, peering upwards into the dense (and to me a little claustrophobic) branches of the pines. It was not long before a low whistle called us to where Valdemar stood, and he pointed: on a branch about six metres above us sat one of the most magnificent birds I had ever seen. It was also one of the meanest-looking birds imaginable. Close-set yellow eyes glared from under angry 'eyebrows' and pronounced facial discs, and its whole demeanour was threatening.

Scarcely daring to breathe, I lined up my telephoto lens, pressed against a tree to steady my hands and shot off several frames. Then, waiting until everyone else had taken their pictures, I crept forward until I was only a few metres from the bird. As it lowered its wings in threat posture, I took a last few shots before backing away, mindful of Valdemar's account of the owl which left long, bloody furrows up the back of a photographer who pushed his luck too far!

After that it was back into the 'chocolate box' scenery of western Norway, the fabulous fiords and magnificent mountains, which are marvellous to look at and to photograph, but which I find a bit aloof and unattainable. On our rather hurried journey north through Norway, I had marked one or two places which I though might repay a closer look on the way back, and one of those was the reserve of Folkstumyren.

The Dovrefjell is a high plateau south of Trondheim. A beautiful wilderness area of mountains, rivers and marshes, it is the home of a great many birds and the most southerly station for some of the real Arctic species. The reserve of Folkstumyren is on Dovrefjell and, as the name suggests, is a large mire or marsh and one of the few places in Norway where cranes breed. When we got there the cranes had already left but the marsh still resounded with the calls of waders, most of them now looking after young. We also found with a sense of great relief that there were no mosquitoes!

The all-seeing wood sandpipers were shouting from the tops of the willow trees in the marsh, vying with dusky or spotted redshanks as to who was sharpest at 'people-spotting'. There is not a chance of going unobtrusively through any area where these birds are breeding!

A snipe got up. It looked large, it didn't 'jig about' in flight like common snipe and it didn't call - it was a great snipe, another new bird for the trip. The great snipe is a summer visitor to Norway and the Baltic provinces, and is hard to come by in Britain, where it is a vagrant winter visitor. This is largely because of its habit of skulking among long vegetation like common snipe. It is quite similar in plumage

opposite: Big, bold and aggressive, the great grey owl is a bird of the forests of Sweden and Finland. It lays its eggs in the disused nests of other forest birds, such as buzzards, and feeds its young on birds and smaller mammals. Fierce in defence of its nest, it has been known to use its talons to rip the clothes - and skin - off the back of anyone approaching its territory.

to common snipe, though when it flies it often shows more white on its tail, and this is a useful identification feature.

A blue-headed wagtail balanced on the end of a twig trying to give a warning 'tseep' with its mouth full of insects. This is one of the continental races of the yellow wagtail *Motacilla flava*, a bird which is widespread in Britain and Europe with several geographic races which can be told apart mainly by head colour.

Willow warblers were singing everywhere. It was easy to see why this little bird is one of the most numerous of the migrants passing through Shetland: Scandinavia is full of them!

One bird had frustrated me for most of the trip. A distinctive, erratic song with some metallic-sounding notes coming from the hidden depths of a thicket had finally been identified as belonging to a bluethroat, surely one of the most beautiful small birds in Scandinavia. It has an iridescent blue gorget with a red 'bull's-eye' spot in the middle. It is also very shy and usually remains hidden in the undergrowth.

At Folkstumyren I came across a pair of bluethroats which were busy catching insects, sometimes flitting up into the air like a flycatcher to intercept craneflies. When the beak could hold no more, they disappeared into the depths of a thicket where presumably they had a well-hidden nest of young. Finally they seemed to accept me as part of the landscape and came within the range of my camera.

The last lap back to Bergen was a sightseeing one via the spectacular coast route, visiting such places as the Briksdal Glacier, and driving over breathtaking mountain roads. We had done a lot of hard motoring through three countries and, although we

Of the four species of skua found in the norther hemisphere, the long-tailed is the smallest and most graceful. It breeds on northern tundra areas of Scandinavia. Its mastery of the air in displays of aerobatics is among the most thrilling sights imaginable. It is bold in defence of its nest and will often land on people's heads to scream protestingly.

Like other skuas it will pursue gulls and terns for food, but on the breeding-grounds it feeds mainly on lemmings.

had by no means seen all of the Scandinavian birds, we had achieved more than I had expected on a first trip.

Now when the wind blows from the south east and I see willow warblers in the garden, or redwings and fieldfares in the Shetland hills, I can visualise the forests and marshes of Scandinavia where these birds have their summer home, and marvel yet again at the skills and abilities with which nature has endowed the birds which must migrate to survive.

Common crane.

5 SHETLAND SUMMER

In recent years, the Shetland summer season has been tainted for many of us by the knowledge that thousands of our sea-birds have failed to raise any young. The worst affected have been birds such as the terns and kittiwakes which feed by catching small fish near the sea surface by shallow plunge-diving. Birds which are able to dive deeply, such as the auks (razorbills, guillemots, puffins and black guillemots) fared better in some areas but have had poor breeding success in others. Black guillemots (tysties) have not been so badly affected, perhaps because they are not so dependent on the pelagic fish such as sand-eels and young *gadoids* (whitefish) but catch more bottom-living fish such butterfish and rockling.

Gannets at Herma Ness.

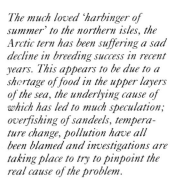

Red-throated divers and shags feed a lot on young saithe and also on sand-eel. The shag population has plummeted in some areas and many divers have failed to raise young. Gannets also feed on shoaling sand-eel, but are able to switch to larger prey such as herring and mackerel if necessary and their population numbers appear reasonably stable.

So what is going wrong, and can anything be done to prevent the situation becoming worse ?

Before I attempt to give my own views on what is a complicated (and locally controversial) subject, perhaps a more general look at our sea-birds and their lifestyles would be appropriate.

Birds which survive the lean days of winter, or have learned to migrate to a suitable wintering place, return to their summer homes to breed. In the tropics where there are only wet and dry seasons and food is available almost all year round, birds do not need to perform extensive migrations, and the breeding season can be prolonged to the point where some birds can be found nesting almost the whole year round. But in the higher latitudes, i.e. nearer to the poles, timing becomes progressively more critical, and the period when food is plentiful becomes shorter.

To balance this, there are more daylight hours available to hasten plant, insect and

The much loved 'harbinger of summer' to the northern isles, the Arctic tern has been suffering a sad decline in breeding success in recent years. This appears to be due to a shortage of food in the upper layers of the sea, the underlying cause of which has led to much speculation; overfishing of sandeels, temperature change, pollution have all been blamed and investigations are taking place to try to pinpoint the real cause of the problem.

plankton growth. This means that the feeding of nestlings has to be much more intensive, and parent birds must work almost round the clock to raise a brood successfully before the icy hand of autumn sends insects into hibernation, covers up seeds and vegetation with ice and snow, or sends the fish out into deeper water.

The Shetland Islands, the most northerly part of the United Kingdom at sixty degrees north, lie well south the true Arctic, but still far enough north that in midsummer the sun only sets for an hour or two. The summer season is consequently shorter than in southern parts of Britain, and the 'timing factor' for breeding birds is that much more critical.

Many of the species which winter outwith the islands time their arrival to coincide with the availability of the type of food to which they are adapted. Small birds such as wheatear and meadow pipits arrive as insects are stirred into motion by the growing heat of the sun, and most of the sea-birds make sure their arrival is synchronised to the hatching or arrival of fish or fish fry.

For the predators this timing is just as critical and this can be seen well in the relationships between the piratical Arctic skua, its usual victim the Arctic tern, and the small fish on which they both depend.

Both Arctic skuas and Arctic terns are known to spend the winter in the southern hemisphere, and the Shetland breeding population probably roams widely over the south Atlantic Ocean. But without the help of clock or compass, the terns will arrive back within a day or two of the same date each year, around 6th May. They will find their enemy the skua already in residence, having arrived a week or so earlier and

Of all the gull tribe the kittiwake is most adapted to a marine life. Only coming to land in order to nest, for most of the year it gets a living by hunting for small surface-swimming fish and other organisms. It is suffering from the same problem as the Arctic tern in Shetland - lack of available food with which to feeds its chicks. As a result, breeding success has been very low in some areas for several years.

practising his piracy harrying kittiwakes or puffins until the terns come back. Occasionally a party of terns may be seen flying past through the 'sounds' between the islands in late April, but these are almost certainly birds heading farther north - perhaps to Iceland or Spitsbergen - and they don't hang about.

Coincident with the arrival of the Arctic terns, swarms of young saithe (called sillocks in Shetland), only two or three centimetres in length, appear close inshore. These will have hatched from spawn laid far offshore, in water as deep as two hundred metres and, having spent their larval stage swimming free in the ocean, they spend the next two, sometimes three years inshore where they form an important part of the food for many sea-birds and also for seals and otters. Two- and three-year-old fish are too large most birds, but have traditionally been an important part of the diet of the Shetland people. Other small fish such as the fry of whiting, herring and sprats and, most importantly, sand-eels play a vital part as the summer progresses and the young terns - and skuas - are all demanding to be fed.

Arctic skuas feed their young on the fish which they rob from the terns, and have become so specialised that they have almost lost the capability of catching food for themselves. This means, of course, that if for any reason the fish don't appear, neither the terns nor the skuas will be able to breed.

To a greater or less extent this applies to all our sea-birds, but some are more vulnerable than others. Some birds can switch to alternative food sources if one should fail and most gulls (with the exception of kittiwake) are good examples of this adaptability.

In Shetland during the last forty years or so when the seine-net fishing for haddock and whiting was profitable, most of the gulls - mainly herring and black-backed gulls in the summer, augmented by glaucous gulls from the north in winter - got a good living by attending the fishing-boats. The catch was usually gutted as soon as it came on board, and the gulls would go in a flock from boat to boat, cleaning up the discards. They sometimes got incredibly bold in the competition for the fish offal; I have seen a fisherman cleaning out the insides of a fish while a gull was hanging on to the tail, tugging frantically in its attempt to get a meal!

If the fishing was dull, the birds would roost in flocks on the nearest headland, leaving a few 'scouts' on watch for fishing activity, sometimes many kilometres away. As soon as a 'lift' of fish was telegraphed in some fashion by the scouts, the whole flock would take flight and head unerringly to wherever the action was.

Among the small land birds, an obvious change in the last half century has been a dramatic turn round in the fortunes of two birds in the bunting family. When I was a boy living on a croft at Aywick, the corn bunting was a familiar bird. Its jangly 'little-bit-of-bread-and-no-cheeeeese' song was heard all summer long, and we used to find its nest among the ryegrass. Now it is probably extinct as a breeding bird in Shetland, and its place has been taken by the reed bunting.

I saw my first reed bunting's nest in 1964 in the marsh between the lochs of Spiggie and Brow, and now in the space of twenty-five years they have successfully colonised the islands, and theirs is the only bunting song that today's Shetland children will know. . .

But to return to sea-birds and the possible causes of the problems they are facing today, we must look back fifty years to the last war in Europe. Fishing effort in the North Sea which had been slowly increasing as engines and gear were developed,

Arctic tern feeding young.

came almost to a standstill during the war and, in consequence, the sea-bird populations flourished as fish stocks increased.

But after the war, increased fishing effort, aided by the development of radar, sonar and all the other manifestations of the 'electronic explosion' put ever-increasing pressures on fish stocks. Combined with the invention of the purse-net, a dangerous stage was reached where the ability to find and catch some species threatened to outstrip the ability of fish to maintain viable populations. Bans had to be imposed on mackerel and herring fishing to allow stocks to recover, and quota systems set up to prevent serious depletion of other fish.

But to my mind even more sinister has been the development of some forms of 'industrial' fishing. This allows the use of small-mesh nets to drag up thousands of small fish which have no direct commercial food value. These are then processed into fish meal to be used mainly for feeding farm animals.

Targeted at species such as Norway pout and sand-eel, the operation undoubtedly also destroys large numbers of immature fish of other kinds like cod, whiting and haddock. The fishing for sand-eels alone has risen until last year (1989) a million tonnes were taken from the North Sea by EEC member countries.

At least two other specific developments could have contributed to the present sea-bird problem. As I mentioned earlier, the saithe or coalfish *Gadus virens* has long been an important fish in Shetland, the surface-shoaling immatures being utilised by many sea-birds. As a human food fish, saithe has never been really popular in Britain and therefore its market value has been low. But now that the North Sea is open to other members of the EEC, the saithe, which is popular especially in France and Germany, is being fished heavily. This could now be having an effect on the numbers of immature fish inshore.

The other development is the fishing of sand-eels in inshore waters round Shetland, which began in earnest in 1974. This small but nutritious fish is used in the manufacture of food for farmed salmon, exported as mink food or converted into fish meal. The yearly catch of sand-eels rose to a peak of 52,000 tonnes in 1982, but then

The great skua (or bonxie, as it is known in Shetland) get its living by harassing other birds into giving up their catch of fish. It will also take the nestlings of other birds and kill adults it is able to catch. It is a summer visitor to Shetland, which is its northern hemisphere headquarters

began to decline until in the present season only some 2,000 tonnes were landed. There is an obvious correlation with the decline in the sea-bird population, and many people are convinced this is the main cause of the problem.

Shetland Bird Club took up the issue and have appealed to the government to curb the fishery, even presenting a petition to the Prime Minister. But although the

The common guillemot is one of the most numerous of the auks. It nests in densely packed colonies on inaccessible cliff-ledges, and except during the breeding season lives out at sea. It is able to dive deeply in search of food so is not quite so restricted as the surface-feeding terns, but it is more vulnerable to pollution of the sea surface and to winter storms.

Ministry has shortened the fishing season a little, licences are still issued allowing local boats to continue the sand-eel fishery. Research has been initiated, both land-based on interactions between the birds and sand-eels, and at sea into the life-cycles of the fish themselves.

My own observations leave me in no doubt that either there are very few sand-eels left in inshore waters (and therefore accessible to feeding sea-birds) or that sand-eels have dramatically changed their habits.

Until recently, you could sit on a Shetland cliff-top in summer and watch the sea-birds - terns, kittiwakes, gulls, auks and sometimes shag - feeding in concentrated groups on or just under the surface of the sea. A closer look - say from a boat - would show that these birds were feeding on sand-eels which were massed in a huge 'ball' just below the surface. This phenomenon has been going on for long enough in Shetland waters for it to be given a local name of 'fuglicaa', which is derived from old Norse 'fugl' meaning bird and 'caa' to drive (as in sheep) - literally a 'bird-drive'.

Sand-eels, as their name suggests, live mainly on sandy sea-beds and actually burrow into the sand, and this 'balling' behaviour near the surface of the sea is a bit of a mystery. Seen from beneath the surface the fuglicaa is a fantastic sight.

Shetland has a long and indented coastline with many fine cliffs and bold headlands which offer secure breeding-places to sea-birds of various kinds. The cliffs on the east side of the little island of Noss are well known as one of the most spectacular 'sea-bird cities' to be seen anywhere. It was here than gannets made their first successful attempts to colonise Shetland. The cliffs are composed of sandstone, a rather soft rock which has been weathered by wind and wave into innumerable nesting niches for several kinds of sea-birds.

Sometimes as big as a house and containing millions of fish, the mass is near spherical. It is in a constant shimmer of glinting silver movement as the countless small fishes swim round and round the outside of the 'ball' and disappear into an orifice within it. After a time (or if disturbed) this living globe breaks up and disappears like a rain of silver back into the depths of the sea.

Some claim that the sand-eels were being chased upwards by predators such as bigger fish, and that they no longer come to the surface because there aren't any big fish left to chase them. I have never found, or heard of, any evidence to support this.

Tony Bomford, a cameraman who was diving from my boat, reported that the water near the 'ball' was 'milky looking' but this is unlikely to be connected with breeding because sand-eels are known to spawn in the sand in winter time.

Whatever the reason for this behaviour, it ensured that the fish became available to surface-feeding birds such as kittiwakes and terns, and the fact is that it no longer happens.

If the reason for the disappearance of the fuglicaa is a natural change in behaviour for whatever reason, then it is not easy to see what can be done about it. But if it can be proven that overfishing of sand-eel is the principal cause of the problem, we can only hope that remedial action can be taken before it is too late for our important sea-bird colonies to recover.

But there are other factors which may be contributing to the lack of small fish in the upper layers of the sea - which is where the main problem seems to lie. There is a great deal of talk nowadays of global warming, the 'greenhouse effect', the destruction of the ozone layer and so on, and it is difficult for an ordinary person to know what is going on, when even the scientists cannot agree. It is only a few years ago that we were being warned about the arrival of another ice age, for heavens' sake! We *are* into a run of milder winters at the moment, and the winter sea temperature is higher than normal, but appears to be still within the range of normal fluctuations. The waters around Shetland depend on the upwelling of currents from the deep Atlantic (the North Atlantic Drift, a tribute of the Gulf Stream) which brings a regular flow of nutrients to the fish spawning and feeding areas. Has there perhaps been a change in the flow or direction of this current?

The build-up of pollutants in the sea has also been blamed. There is no doubt that instead of treating the sea as the giver of life to mankind, as it certainly is, it has for far too long been treated as the world's sewer. Chemical effluent from industrial operations, nitrates from the excessive use of chemical fertilisers, and sewage waste from an ever-increasing human population all eventually leach into the sea. We read of epidemics in seal populations in the Baltic and southern North Sea, and even among bearded seals in the White Sea off northern Russia. We hear of mysterious deaths of whales and dolphins on the Scottish coast, and of the virtual disappearance of sea-trout from some of their west coast rivers. Headlines scream of algal blooms which destroy fish farms in Norway, and radio broadcasts give official warnings not to eat shellfish from some areas of the British coasts.

There are 'hidden' factors about which we can only speculate, such as the direct effects on sand-eel stocks from the greatly increased shoals of herring and mackerel which are the result of recent bans on fishing for these species. Does anyone really know what effects the radioactive fall-out following the disaster at the nuclear plant at Chernobyl had on the food chain of the sea?

I find it very difficult to dwell on these serious - even gloomy - thoughts when the sun is shining, the winds light and I have been asked to take a party of visitors out for a boat trip. There are plenty of birds to be seen: near the salmon cages a red-throated diver patters along the surface with its feet as it gets airborne. A sizable saithe dangling from its beak indicates another meal for its young up on the hill loch beyond the village. Even if the saithe has been reared on salmon pellets, I am sure the young 'rain goose' won't mind.

Great Black-backed gull chasing a puffin.

As the sea is calm I turn in to a narrow cleft on the headland, cutting the engine and gliding in between the faces of grey rock to let my passengers get the flavour of the sights and sounds of a Shetland geo.

Fulmars cackle beneath the waving blue heads of sheepsbit and several downy young peer at us with fathomless black eyes. A pair of tysties are displaying at each other on a ledge, their high-pitched calls extending even beyond our human audio range, judging by the soundless opening of vermilion-lined beaks.

The tide is low and someone points excitedly into the clear water to where a couple of large sea-urchins are making their sedate way along the rock-face. I point out the empty 'shells' of others on the grassy cliff-top, and explain that this is the work of the local great black-backed gulls, who seem to enjoy cracking open these echinoderms (which are really modified starfish) to get at the small amount of 'meat' inside.

We carefully skirt the small island of Kayholm where I know there are a couple of otter holts, and if is a lucky day we might find one out fishing. No luck this time, only a couple of redshanks take fright and fly off yelping in alarm, and a female merganser swims among the thongweed, head poking under the water to look for small fish.

I open the throttle a bit and head out into the sound, where the tide flows strongly and it is a favoured feeding place for auks. Sure enough, we soon come up to a party of puffin and a single guillemot. I cut the engine again and let the boat drift towards the birds while my passengers admire the curious beaks. 'They are much smaller than I expected' is the usual remark from people seeing puffins for the first time.

One surfaces nearby with several small fishes dangling from its beak. I wait for the inevitable question. 'But how does it catch the last fish without losing those its already caught?'

I give my usual answer: that it probably all happens as the bird is 'flying' at top speed underwater, and that the pressure of the water holds the fish already caught against the bird's sharp mandibles while it snaps up another in a fraction of a second.

A single porpoise rolls over near the boat, causing some excitement, and I advise people not to use binoculars to watch for its reappearance. A porpoise never appears where you expect it to! Its local Shetland name is 'neesick', which means 'the sneezer', referring to the explosive exhalation of breath it gives as it surfaces for air. I am pleased to see the porpoise, because they too have been affected by the general shortage of food recently, and have not been easy to find in their usual haunts.

We approach the island of Hascosay at its south-western extremity; the water there is deep enough to take the boat into the geo where the shags and rock doves nest. Sure enough, a couple of rock doves fly out of the crack with a clatter of wings, and we can see a scarcely fledged youngster perched on a ledge in the gloom of the sea-cave. Rock doves are the natural ancestors to most of the feral pigeons which are an often unwelcome feature of many towns and cities. It is only on the more remote cliffs and islands that they have escaped the degradation of interbreeding with man-manipulated colour forms, and retain the true original plumage.

A dozen shags and a cormorant are perched on a stack nearby and, as usual, the cormorant is the first to 'chicken out' and fly off as we approach. But it sits long enough for me to point out the difference between the two species. The cormorant has a heavier build, less upright stance and - as this is an immature - a pale chest, while the shag (minus its crest now in midsummer) looks more scrawny and is relatively longer-necked. Shags come into breeding plumage as early as January, growing a

substantial 'shaving-brush' crest on the head. This is lost soon after laying commences in April or early May - which is a shame, because most people visit the seabird colonies in summer, and so rarely see a shag in all its glory.

As the 'laar' (breath) of wind is from the south east, I head slowly up the western shore, knowing that, with the ebbing tide, there will be a few seals hauled out on the rocks. I approach slowly so that the animals will not be taken by surprise and panic into a rush for the sea, but even so several of the younger seals take fright and slide into the water. My 'old' boat was well known to the local seals, and they would allow a really close approach, but I have only had my present boat a couple of years and they are still suspicious.

All except one are common seals and, as the autumn moult approaches, they show the usual variation of colours. The largest animals are quite brown in their worn coats, especially after they have dried out on the rocks, while the young born this year are still dark greyish-black. But all have the finely spotted skin and distinctive headshape that denotes our race of *Phoca vitulina*.

The one exception is a larger animal with a pale creamy front covered in dark blotches, a long nose and a steely grey back. It is a female grey seal, probably pregnant but not due to have her pup until late September.

It is a good opportunity to point out the differences between the two species, and we drift in until the seals get restless; it is the grey who rolls into the water first.

I start up the engine again and move on, staying within fifty metres of the shore, which is the usual feeding range of the local otters. A party of turnstone fly off the beach below the house. A few (mainly immature) birds usually summer in Shetland, but as this party contains one or two individuals still in summer plumage, they are probably early arrivals - perhaps failed breeders - from the north.

Everyone is keen to see otter, but again they prove elusive and we round the north of the island with nothing other than a few passing gannet, some tysties and shags and a couple of rabbits spotted among the peaty banks.

It is a passenger who spots the otter. Not, as I expected, fishing in the sea but ambling with its rather ungainly gait along the top of the bank. I immediately stop the engine and we drift parallel to the animal as it makes its way down the beach and into the sea. I suspect it has either seen or heard us, and this is confirmed by the fact that it just doesn't appear again. I know of no animal of its size which can disappear so completely as an otter!

Everyone is delighted to have had a glimpse of this most elusive and rare of British mammals, and there are smiles all round as we move on. Rounding the east side of the island the sea gets a little choppier in the tideway but we have a grandstand view of a gannet being robbed by a great skua. After forcing the gannet down on to the sea, the skua just doesn't let it get airborne again until it has vomited up its cropful of fish.

An Arctic skua flies lazily past, then suddenly accelerates as it spots a party of puffins heading north towards Hermaness. After a frantic few minutes' chase the skua realises this isn't going to be cost-effective and breaks off to look for something easier. If the skua can make an approach from 'below and behind' (like the wartime fighter pilots!), there is a chance that the surprised puffin will drop the fish it is carrying. But if the puffin is aware of the pirate in good time, it can accelerate to a speed the skua cannot match.

So our circumnavigation of Hascosay continues, past Oxnageo and the stack called the Grey-bearded Man, through the gap inside the notorious reef called the

opposite: *Among the many beautiful scenes on the Shetland coastline, I rate the north side of the island of Fetlar highly. As it is only a hour's boat ride from home, I never tire of exploring this area in summer or winter. Its grassy slopes are home to puffins, shearwaters, storm petrels and myriads of fulmar. Grey seals breed on the boulder beaches below the cliffs, which are pounded by autumn storms, and huge pollack, saithe and other tasty fish lurk around the rocky sea bottom nearby.*

The boat in the photograph is my twenty-eight foot (nine metre) Fyvie 'Consort', which provided my sea transport for over twenty years.

Baas of Hascosay, the graveyard of a number of ships, and back to our moorings in Mid Yell. We haven't set the world alight, but we have seen a selection of the many kinds of birds and animals which choose to make Shetland their home.

A human life-span is but a blip on the screen of evolution, and the current sea-bird problems may be little more than that. On the other hand they may be a serious indication that man is - as many people insist - doing irreparable damage to our own fuglicaa, the earth.

6 THE NORTH ATLANTIC ISLANDS

If you spend your life on one island or in one place, it is all too easy to become parochial in your outlook, and to think that the world begins and ends there in your back garden. I have long been a avid reader of books about islands. My bookshelves contain well-thumbed copies of books by authors such as Lockley, Williamson, Atkinson, Kearton and Fraser-Darling, to name but a few dedicated island-lovers. But however enjoyable, reading about islands is nowhere near as rewarding as visiting them, and I consider myself fortunate in having been able to spend some time on the north Atlantic islands of Iceland, the Faroe Islands and that most remote of the British islands, St Kilda.

Iceland

The largest and most northerly is Iceland which, although its name might suggest an Arctic situation, actually lies south of the Arctic Circle. That imaginary line just touches the tiny island of Grimsey, Iceland's most northerly outpost.

Iceland is one of the youngest islands in the world: when the first primates were already clambering through the African jungles, a cataclysmic volcanic eruption of part of the mid-Atlantic fault line brought a whole new land-mass into being. This, called the Thulean Province, covered much of what we now call the north Atlantic Ocean, but over thousands of years, much of it sank again beneath the waters.

During another epoch, the polar ice-cap expanded and covered a large part of the northern hemisphere, and it was only when that receded about 12,000 years ago that

Iceland is a haven for wildfowl: the many rich, shallow lakes and ponds have an abundance of insect larvae, which suits growing ducklings. This family of tufted ducks was photographed on Lake Tjørnin in the middle of the capital, Reykjavik!

One of the most evocative sounds of the northern tundra is the liquid, piping call of the golden plover. In summer plumage the bird sports a black front outlined in white, and it is a feature of Icelandic birds that the black is clearly delineated from the white. In more southerly populations the black front is often suffused with paler markings, particularly on the neck and 'face'.

what was left of the Thulean Province reappeared from beneath the ice as the island we now call Iceland. Just over 100,000 square kilometres in extent, Iceland is still largely barren and battered from its fiery birth, and the landscape continues to be shaped and racked by volcanoes. About seventy-three per cent of the island is covered by glaciers, ice-caps or barren lava fields, and man's attempts at cultivating and utilising the land are confined to low-lying deltas or river valleys near the sea.

Over 250,000 people live in Iceland today, making their living mainly from fishing and farming in the coastal areas.

My first visit to 'the daughter of fire' was back in the summer of 1969, when with two friends, Ian and Marie Brooker, we set sail from the port of Leith on the old mail steamer 'Gullfoss', and after several days of not too comfortable travelling, we had our first glimpse of Iceland.

The eider duck is widespread and in places abundant around coastal areas of Iceland. In late summer the males leave the female to look after the ducklings, and they gather in great flocks to undergo their summer moult. This is only a part of a huge flock just beginning to lose its breeding plumage.

I had to admit my first impression was not quite what I had expected: instead of bold cliffs and mountain peaks, all we could see from the heaving deck of the boat was a seemingly endless beach of black shingle fringed by white breakers. Then I became aware that the bank of white clouds beyond was in reality the great ice-cap of Vatnajökull. A surge of adrenalin banished the early morning queasiness, and the feeling of excitement came back as we examined this new land through binoculars.

After arrival at the capital of Reykjavik we watched in some trepidation as our heavily laden Landrover was swung out on a derrick and deposited on the quay, but all went well and as soon as we had cleared customs we set out to take a look at this bright little capital city.

In the middle of Revkjavik is a small lake called Lake Tjörnin which has become a centre piece to the city. It is a good example of the way birds will take advantage of what man can provide, once they are confident they will not be molested.

Here was a variety of wildfowl, some of them with broods of young, all scrabbling after scraps of bread provided by shoppers and passers-by. Eider ducks were vying with mallard and tufted ducks, the ducklings dodging in and around people's legs. Adult greylag geese were more aloof and watched anxiously as their goslings joined in the competition for food. Scaup, long-tailed duck, tufted duck and even the rare Barrow's goldeneye were all there and, most importantly, were there of their own free will.

We were told that in winter when the lake is frozen, a large part is kept ice-free by directing water from the town's hot water supply, and even the wild whooper swans come in to take advantage of the food offered.

I also wished to pay my respects to the Curator of the Natural History Museum, the late Finnur Gudmundsson, who had been so helpful in planning the trip.

Eventually we headed out of the city and got the feel of the lunar landscape by visiting the area of hot springs at Hveragerði which not only supplies Reykjavik with all the hot water for centrally heating houses, but heats the swimming-pools and greenhouses as well.

We realised straight away that the Landrover was a good choice of vehicle because

Black-tailed Godwit.

even the main roads were pretty rough, and we intended spending most of our time in the north of the island where road and track conditions promised to be even worse. The roads were usually wide enough for two vehicles to pass without slowing down, but in dry weather this meant enveloping each other in a cloud of choking lava dust. If it was really wet and the oncoming vehicle was a large lorry, we were sprayed with a glutinous mud which windscreen-wipers only managed to smear further!

But the landscape became grander and more exciting as we drove north; great fiords cut deep into the land, and mountain-sides of lava screes towered away up into the clouds. Where the road passed through the coastal plains there were farms with cattle grazing on knee-high grass. The bubbling song of whimbrel mingled with the excited yelping of breeding redshank could be heard whenever we stopped for a break.

Both these waders are summer visitors to Iceland and are widespread and common on the coastal grassland flats. The whimbrel is the Arctic version of the curlew and is distributed circumpolarly round the 'tundra belt' or uplands. The Iceland population probably winters in Iberia or North Africa. As both breed in Shetland, I was quite familiar with their appearance and their calls.

Iceland gull in winter.

Nearer the shores, we could see parties of eider ducks with broods of ducklings. Iceland has a huge population of eider and we were to see some large flocks further north.

I had imagined that the coast would be largely cliff-bound, but in fact cliffs suitable for sea-birds are not common except around the far northern headlands. So it was not until we set out to explore the headland of Snaefellsness that we encountered sea-birds in any numbers.

Kittiwakes were by far the most numerous of the gulls, nesting in huge noisy colonies on precipitous cliffs, while glaucous gulls with their all pale wing-tips replaced the herring gulls and black-backs I had become used to seeing in Shetland.

It was at Snaefellsness that I saw the bird I had hoped to find - and which was 'new' to me - the Brünnich's guillemot. In America it is called the thick-billed murre, and it is closely related to the common guillemot which breeds in large numbers on the cliffs of Shetland. The plumage of both species follows the same general pattern of dark above and white below, though the Brünnich's is always more intensely black on the upper parts, and the stubbier beak, with a clear white mark along the upper mandible, is the distinctive feature which is most obvious on this northern relative. Brünnichs nest in a similar fashion to our common guillemot, packed shoulder to shoulder on cliff ledges.

Nesting nearby in holes in the boulder were a colony of puffins, and I probably imagined that these Icelandic birds looked larger than those nesting in Shetland, because I knew that studies had shown this to be the case. What I certainly wouldn't see in Shetland were snow buntings carrying food in below the same boulders as the puffins, while their mates sang their lovely wild song from the top.

Where the great rivers of molten lava had flowed in the distant past was now a jumbled mass of solidified rock-like structures which sometimes stretched for many kilometres. Much of this *hraun*, as it is called in Iceland, is moss-covered and liable to break off underfoot; it is very hard on boots - and ankles! It is a fine habitat for wild flowers: in many places mountain avens forms great carpets of blooms, and many species of saxifrage, dwarf shrubs and other Arctic-Alpine specialities can be seen.

We had spent an hour or two in the *hraun* and had stopped for a rest when a huge white-tailed eagle came flying past. We wondered what it was doing so far from the coastal cliffs, but we learned later that they sometimes build their eyries on inland lava pinnacles.

In Shetland a number of pairs of the white-tailed sea-eagle used to nest in the high cliffs, but in the late nineteenth century they went into a decline and the last pair nested in 1914. It is generally believed that persecution by man was the main reason for the extinction of this magnificent bird as a breeding species in Shetland. About this time the species was in danger of extinction in Iceland also, but legislation to protect the bird was passed and the eagles survived. But only just: still today the population numbers only in the region of fifty pairs.

After spending a few days at Snaefellsness, our final goal was the fabulous Lake Mývatn. Mention to almost any European bird-watcher that you are going to Iceland and the response will be 'You must go to Mývatn!'

In Britian the ptarmigan is a bird of the high mountain plateaux of the north, but in Iceland it can be found breeding at all levels. It is the only member of the grouse family to live here. The hen lays up to a dozen eggs and can be quite bold in attacking intruders.

Black-tailed Godwit stretching.

The fourth largest lake in Iceland, it lies in the middle of an area of intense geothermal and volcanic activity, and its thirty-seven square kilometres of water surface provide a summer home to large numbers of waterfowl.

It has been estimated that over 10,000 duck of fifteen different species breed round the margins and islands of the lake, as well as whooper swans, great northern and red-throated divers, Slavonian grebes and greylag geese. Red-necked phalarope are very numerous, and waders such as whimbrel, redshank and black-tailed godwit nest in the meadows nearby It is not too unusual to see a magnificent gyr falcon swoop across the lake on a hunting expedition - and with a wide choice of birds on the menu!

Lake Mývatn has the privilege of being the only European breeding station for Barrow's goldeneye, a duck of American origin, and in the River Laxa which flows from Mývatn to the sea, you are assured of seeing the beautiful Harlequin duck, another New World species which also has its only European outpost here. To the keen birdwatcher these two species alone are worth an expedition.

The name Mývatn means 'midge lake' and the principal reason the lake supports a large population of birds and fish is the astronomical numbers of chironomid and simuliid larvae which hatch out in the clear water. Important as they may be to the birds and trout, they can be very annoying to humans and, although they may not bite, the sheer numbers of midges and blackflies have been known to send birdwatchers - and particularly photographers - into paroxysms of rage and frustration.

But it is still a wonderful place to visit. The insects are only an annoyance on the rare days when there isn't a breeze blowing, and are more than compensated for by the wealth of bird life in the area And it is not only birds. There is lots to interest the botanist, from the stately 'Queen of Mývatn' to orchids such as northern green and small white, and much more.

On that first visit to Iceland we made Lake Mývatn our turning point, but before retracing our route back to Reykjavik and the ferry, we made a detour up the valley of Bárðardalur to look for one of the breeding places of the pink-footed goose. This is one of the group of 'grey geese' which is well known as a wintering bird on the

overleaf, right:
While most of Iceland's birds have European or 'old world' origins, there are two members of the duck family that are from the American continent. These are the Barrow's goldeneye and the harlequin, which is the one pictured. They like to spend much of their time in fast rivers such as the Laxa, which flows from Lake Mývatn to the sea. They winter on the coast and seem to prefer rocky shores and breaking surf to quieter waters.

mainland of Britain, and almost the whole of the European population breeds in Iceland. The sites they choose for nesting are the steep-sided inland gorges and cliffs formed by the rivers which rush down to the sea from the great ice-caps. We followed the road up the valley, crossing and recrossing over bridges which became progressively more primitive until finally they ceased to exist and the track disappeared into the river to reappear at the far bank. We presumed this to be a regular ford and drove across with the water slopping in over the floor of the Land rover, but we eventually made it up on to the high inland plateau.

Although we found the geese, the nests were long deserted and the large creches of goslings were big enough to run much faster than we could.

We allowed a day or two for sightseeing along the south coast, visiting the historic parliament site of Tingvellir, the magnificent waterfall of Gullfoss and the spouting hot springs of Geysir. The name comes from the old Norse word meaning 'to gush' and was not only given to the township nearby, but got into the English language as a descriptive name for any jet of water.

Since the advent of a car-ferry system connecting Denmark, Norway, Shetland, Faroe and Iceland, it has become easier for me to take a vehicle over and, because the ferry terminus in Iceland is in one of the eastern fiords called Seyðisfjördur, this has given me the opportunity of exploring the north and east coast of Iceland in greater detail.

There have been many memorable moments: watching a gyr falcon trying to out-manoeuvre puffins in flight off the headland of Tjörnes; finding purple sandpipers, dunlin, redshank and Arctic terns all breeding together near Núpscatla; the spectacular east coast road which in places cuts across forty-five degree mountain slopes where

Gyr Falcon chasing a golden plover.

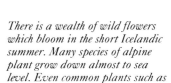

There is a wealth of wild flowers which bloom in the short Icelandic summer. Many species of alpine plant grow down almost to sea level. Even common plants such as this bog cotton have their own quiet beauty when backlit by the evening sun.

you can look down on vast flocks of moulting eider drakes on the sea below. On to the camp-site at Scaftafjell where ptarmigan forage among the tents and the dried-up river-bed is ablaze with yellow and pink stonecrop, intensely blue Alpine gentians and the beautifully named 'Arctic river beauty' an *epilobium* which is one of my all-time favourite flowers.

Iceland is an island of great character which always produces something new and exciting. I look forward to returning again and again.

The Faroe Islands

The young puffin stopped preening tufts of grey down from its feathers, stood on tiptoe and flapped its growing wings vigorously, sending a small shower of dandruff-like particles across the wooden table. It then defecated delicately between the sugar bowl and a coffee cup, settled down with a yawn and appeared to go to sleep.

'You are a naughty bird, Eyvør' said the Birdman, pointing to the dropping with the stem of his pipe. 'But then, you do not know any better.'

He got up to fetch a cloth to wipe the tiny mess, at the same time bringing another strip of herring which Eyvør accepted daintily before tucking its small unpuffin-like beak into its back feathers and dozing off again. The characteristic gaudy beak of the puffin is but a summer adornment, and is shed in winter. Young birds also have quite a small black beak during their first winter.

It was difficult to believe that the Birdman (I never did learn his name) was the same man I had watched earlier in the day catching puffins on the cliffs beyond the village. He was perched precariously on the very edge of the precipice waiting for puffins to fly past, and when one came within reach he swung his long-handled *fleygastong* (which is like a landing-net on the end of a four-metre pole) to intercept the bird. If he was lucky and the bird ended up in the net, the Birdman would extract it and, with a deft flick, break its neck before adding it to others in a canvas bag carried round his waist.

The puffin is one of the easiest birds to identify with its unmistakable 'beak of many colours' and there are many large colonies, especially round the north of Iceland and in the Faroe Islands. In Faroe they have traditionally been used for food and are still on the menu in restaurants in Torshavn. They have been declining in recent years and it is believed this is due to a shortage of the small fish on which they feed, rather than the attentions of the fowlers.

But, sitting in the wood-panelled living-room of the Birdman's house on the little island of Mykines, listening to his tales of the sea and of the exploits of the Faroese fowlers of old, I could think of no reason why he should be considered any more hard or cruel than anyone who has ever eaten a chicken joint, a hamburger - or even a fish-finger!

It was late August and the first south-easterly gale of the season was blowing strongly over Mykines, crashing into the rocky 'geo' which is the island's only landing-place. Cascades of salt spray had already washed some of the kittiwakes' nests off the lower ledges when we took a last look out before nightfall, and there seemed little chance that the old 'Sulan' would be able to make a landing tomorrow, even if the sea conditions allowed a crossing from Sørvágur. But here, under the thick turf roof and the stone walls which had weathered many a north Atlantic gale, we were secure from the driving rain, and the heaviest gusts of wind did little more than make the oil-lamp flicker in its hanger.

Some three hundred kilometres in a north-westerly direction, the Faroe Islands are roughly the same distance from Shetland as are Aberdeen to the south and Bergen in Norway to the east. But although we are almost close neighbours, communication between the two island groups have never been easy until comparatively recently.

At one time sharing the old Norn language, even there we had been forced to diverge, because while Shetland became absorbed into Scotland and obliged to take on the Scots/English language, the Faroese managed to retain and develop their own language, using that of their 'parent' country Denmark as the second tongue. Much the same happened in a general cultural sense, with Faroe becoming even more independent and determined to maintain its old customs.

This is seen in the way the Faroese people fiercely defend their traditional rights to hunt birds and animals for food, and their resentment of the people who come from more 'enlightened' countries to try and point out the 'error of their ways' to the islanders.

There are of course arguments on both sides. . .

Conservationists claim that traditions - no matter how old or well-established - which add unnecessary pressures to species which are already in danger, can no longer be justified in a modern world, and should be abandoned. They point out that the Faroese are generally well off and no longer need to hunt pilot whales or puffins to exist, and that the practice has become something of a sport rather than a necessity. They will also say that the Faroese method of killing whales is a barbarous way of treating an intelligent, warm-blooded mammal.

The Faroese (well, most of them) maintain that those who oppose their traditional ways are people who have never had to hunt and kill to survive, who are happy to let other people 'do the dirty work' and to buy their meat ready-packaged from a supermarket; that whale- and bird-hunting are community activities which help foster a 'community spirit' and that the birds and animals are all used for human food. They also insist that hunting is not done for sport, as it is in many 'sophisticated' countries, although they may admit that all forms of traditional hunting take on a certain glamour, especially in the minds of the younger men. They will also claim that the hunting of sea-birds is very strictly controlled, and that they only take out 'surplus' birds which would probably not survive the winter anyway.

As an islander I can see something of both points of view, and I have been aware of a sense of embarrassment in some of my Faroese friends that the outside world should think of them as 'barbarians'. It would be infinitely better if these feelings could be translated into action by the islanders themselves, rather than imposed by outsiders who, by their very upbringing, may never fully understand the ways of islanders.

We had crossed over to Mykines early in the day, sailing down the long fiord from the village of Sørvágur. We gazed in wonderment at the fantastic shape of the small island of Tindholmur as we passed. Flat, green and verdant on one side, the other rises skyward for nearly three hundred metres like a vast cathedral spire. This is said to have been the scene of the Faroese legend of the eagle and the baby. Unlike the Shetland version where the baby was rescued by a young lad who later married the lass he had saved from death, the Faroese story is one of heroism but sadness, where the mother climbed to the eyrie (which no man had ever been able to do) only to find that her baby was dead.

Mykines has some similarities to Foula in Shetland: they are both the farthest westerly island of the group, largely cliff-bound and lacking a good, all-weather landing-place. While Foula has a population of about forty people nowadays, Mykines has fewer than a score of permanent residents, all living in a tight group of picturesque turf-roofed cottages situated on the cliff-top above the landing-place.

A jutting headland called Mykineshólmur, covered in good grass, is separated from the main island by a narrow chasm called Hólmgjógv through which the sea growls and rushes. Early this century an iron bridge was constructed to span the gap and therefore make accessible not only large areas of good grazing, but a vast colony of puffins and other sea-birds including the only Faroese gannet colony.

As our plans only allowed for one day on Mykines, we made the *hølmur* our main target, and after leaving our things in the empty house in which we had arranged to spend the night, we set off to follow the steep cliff path which leads to the bridge.

Drake Barrow's Goldeneye.

There were puffins everywhere: the sky was full of whirring wings, and hundreds of birds were standing around on the grassy slope which was honeycombed with puffin burrows. We could hear the guttural growling of still more coming from underground burrows. It was difficult to believe that these birds had been harvested for food on Mykines for generations, or to argue against the Faroese claim that the strict regulations which apply to the fowling are designed to ensure that the population numbers are not adversely affected.

The bridge across the *gjógv* seemed very slender and a long way above the sea surging below, but we made our way safely across and walked out to the end of the *hølmur* to where we could overlook the gannet colony.

I could have been back on Hermaness in Shetland. There they sat, big beautiful birds with snowy white plumage offset by buff heads and black wing-tips. They had built their usual untidy nests less than a metre apart on the steep ledges, and now in August each nest held a large, fluffy young gannet. Some were already sprouting feathers and were busily preening the new growth, some were sleeping off their last feed of fish, while others were food-begging from every bird within reach.

It was this colony of gannets that in 1860 was joined by a black-browed albatross, a lost wanderer from the southern oceans. Every year for thirty-four years it came back, earning itself the name of *súlukongur* - 'king of the gannets' - till finally on 11th May 1894, it was shot. The skin ended up in the Natural History Museum in

The tiny island of Mykines is the westernmost of the Faroe group. Its very small resident population lives in the attractive village with its turf-roofed houses. Traditionally the turves were placed on a base of overlapping 'tiles' of birch bark, which made the roof impervious to water. The thick turf also provides very good insulation and I can testify that the houses are very comfortable - even in a howling gale!

Copenhagen and it was only when the corpse was examined that it was discovered that súlukongur was in fact a female!

The weather had changed by afternoon, with a strong breeze from the south east and the sniff of an approaching rain front in the air. We made our way back across the bridge through the huge puffin colony of *lundaland* to our comfortable turf-roofed house for a much needed meal.

Eyvør woke up and made food-begging noises, so the Birdman finished his story and cut up some more strips of herring which he fed to the little bird. He explained that the young puffin had been found wandering in the village with a damaged wing, probably having been mauled by one of the many cats in the neighbourhood (most of whom, incidentally, have six toes on each foot) and he said that he would look after Eyvør for some weeks until it was well enough to be released.

'But,' I said, 'wouldn't it have been simpler just to have snapped its neck?'

The Birdman looked hurt and stroked the head of the now sleeping bird.

'But I like puffins,' he said.

There was really no answer to that. . .

St Kilda

Often called 'Britain's loneliest outpost', the small island group of St Kilda lies nearly eighty kilometres west of the Hebrides in Scotland, out in the storm-tossed waters of the north Atlantic Ocean. That it has been populated from prehistoric times is evidenced by the remains of neolithic buildings, mainly on Hirta, the largest island in the group. One can only guess who these earliest settlers may have been, but the existence of Norse as well as Gaelic place-names suggests that the islands were

known to the Vikings. Indeed, the name 'St Kilda' is something of a mystery, as no saint of that name is known and the name is probably a corruption. The earliest known map calls the group 'S.Kilda', and in the old Norse language the name 'Kelda' means 'spring' or 'well', so it seems possible that the islands, which do have a number of freshwater springs, were used as a watering-place by the Vikings when they were involved in their warlike raiding and invasions of the northern parts of Britain.

Whether St Kilda has been occupied continuously since early times is open to conjecture, but the earliest comprehensive account of the islands and their people was written by Martin Martin in 1697. He was employed as literary tutor to the

above: The most remote of the British islands, St Kilda was populated until 1930, when the dwindling number of folk requested that they should be evacuated and re-settled. This is the settlement of Village Bay seen from the little island of Dún, which provides partial shelter to the landing-place in most weather, except south-easterly gales.

left: The rounded 'beehive'-shaped structures seen dotted over the slopes of St Kilda are called cleits. They were used for storage by the islanders, not only for food such as mutton and birds, but also for peat for firing and hay for the animals.

The name 'St Kilda' is a bit of a puzzle. No saint of that name is known, and the name Kilda is most likely 'kelda', the old Norse word for well or spring. The island was known to the Vikings and was probably used as a watering-place. It was most likely they who introduced - perhaps unwittingly - the field mouse which in its subsequent isolation has developed into a separate race.

McLeods of Dunvegan, who claimed ownership of St Kilda. He recorded the simple lifestyle of the islanders, and described their legendary prowess as cragsmen, imposed no doubt by their almost total dependence upon sea-birds for food.

As salt would have been a precious commodity, all their meat had to be air-dried in order to preserve it for the winter months, and this was done by the use of *cleits*. These were beehive-shaped stone structures, made so that the many apertures between the stones let the wind through, with most of the moisture being trapped on the rough surfaces of the stones. The roofs were made of turf and were waterproof. As dry air has curative properties, any meat or fish hung in the *cleits* dried off without going rotten and would then 'keep' for months.

The same system was used in Shetland in the old days (they were called 'skeos') and in the Faroes a modernised version is still in everyday use. Every St Kildan family owned a number of *cleits* and they were scattered all over the island, many of them convenient to the bird cliffs because 'fresh' birds were much heavier than those that had dried out, and everything had to be carried back to the village eventually.

When Martin visited the island, the population numbered 180 but there was a gradual decline until by 1930 there were fewer than forty people left. There had been bad harvests and disastrous storms, the spirit of the islanders was broken and they petitioned the government to help them leave St Kilda for good.

28th August 1930 was a sad day, as the islanders closed their doors for the last time. They boarded the SS 'Dunara Castle' to start a new life on the mainland, leaving their island home to the seals and sea-birds.

Storm petrels.

After the evacuation the owner, Sir Reginald McLeod, sold the island to the Marquis of Bute who was particularly interested in preserving St Kilda as a bird sanctuary. On his death in 1956 the island was bequeathed to the National Trust for Scotland.

I had long wanted to visit St Kilda, and the opportunity of at least *seeing* the islands came when I was invited to join a National Trust cruise as a lecturer and sort of 'general helper'.

The day scheduled for the circumnavigation of St Kilda dawned with a thick sea-fog blanketing out everything. Even the sea was scarcely visible from up on the bridge deck. Several hundred passengers lined the ship's rails, staring into the fog and willing it to clear.

The National Trust staff in the cruise office were no less anxious. They knew that a number of passengers had joined the cruise just to see St Kilda, and that they would almost be made to feel responsible for any disappointment.

On the bridge the atmosphere was tense; the sweeping cursor of the radar showed the nearest of the islands, Levenish, to be only a kilometre distant and, although the water was deep enough, there comes a point beyond which no prudent captain will take a liner full of passengers.

Now with the engines at 'slow ahead' the ship nosed in, keeping Levenish on the port bow. Gannets and fulmars appeared out of the mist, flew alongside for a few minutes and disappeared again. A party of puffins had to take evasive action as they nearly flew into the side of the ship.

And then it happened!

The fog seemed to part without warning, revealing the great headland of Rhuaival over three hundred metres above us, mist trailing like smoke from its peak and even a stray beam of sunshine lighting up the craggy outlines of the cliffs.

It was a moment of sheer magic. No theatre producer could have dreamed up a more dramatic introduction. A spontaneous cheer went round the ship, followed by a babble of talk as everyone relaxed.

The captain came in from the wing of the bridge with a hint of a smile on his usually rather stern face. He produced a snowy handkerchief from his pocket and wiped his eyes. 'Bloody fog makes your eyes water,' he said to no-one in particular.

St Kilda never does things by halves: the whole setting is one of high drama. The cliffs are the highest in Britain, it is our most remote inhabited island and it holds the biggest gannet colony in the world.

Yes, it is inhabited again, only this time by an army detachment which monitors the efforts of a missile range in the Hebrides, but it does mean that electric light and other amenities are made available - including a pub called the Puff Inn! The National Trust for Scotland have an on-going programme of work on the island, keeping the cottages of the former islanders in a good state of repair, maintaining a small museum and generally ensuring that St Kilda and the St Kildans will never be forgotten.

I joined one of the work-parties and helped rebuild *cleits* and repair storm damage around the cottages. But I wanted to get the atmosphere and 'feel' of the place. To imagine what it would have been like a hundred years ago, when men were swinging over the cliffs on ropes made of horsehair, and climbing the soaring pinnacles of Stac

The suspension bridge which spans the cleft of Hólmgjógv makes accesible not only the lighthouse on Mykineshólmur, but several acres of good grass and thousands of puffins which are cropped for human food.

opposite: About three hundred metres above the sea, the Lovers' Stone is mentioned in literature as the place where St Kildan youths had to prove their manhood. The test was to stand on one foot on the very edge of the rock and place the heel of the other foot against the toe of the first. Then the clenched fists had to be placed in front of the second foot, one in front of the other. Few people can do it on a chair, far less a rock three hundred metres up in the air!

Lee and Stac an Armin to harvest the *gugas*, the young gannets which would ensure they survived the next winter.

I climbed to the top of Conachair and Mullagh Mør and was choked with emotion at the cliffscapes and the interplay of sun on sea and land. I joined a party to climb down the great west cliffs to the boulder scree of Carn Mør, where we stayed until darkness fell and listened to the calls of Manx shearwater, Leach's and storm petrels as they came in from the ocean to feed their young, hidden deep under the boulders.

These three members of the *Procellariidae* family have one thing in common: they are all 'night birds', only coming in to the screes and grassy slopes of the cliffs under

The cliffs of St Kilda are among the finest in Britain and contain huge numbers of breeding sea-birds in the summer. Manx shearwaters are related to the fulmar and the little storm petrel and, like the latter, are nocturnal at the breeding grounds, coming in to relieve their mate on the nest and only under cover of darkness.

cover of darkness to change places with their mate on the single egg, deep within a burrow, or later to feed the young.

The Manx shearwater is the largest of the three, and looks like a small black and white fulmar (to which it is, of course, related). They nest in loose colonies on the more remote islands to the west and north of Britain, and also in Faroe and Iceland. Leach's petrel is the rarest and least well known of the three, with the largest British population on St Kilda. Smallest of the three is the storm petrel, a sparrow-sized sea-bird sailors used to call 'Mother Carey's Chicken'. In daylight they are only to be seen from ships at sea, when the two smaller petrels appear all dark birds with white rumps as they flutter and dance across the waves. Leach's has a forked tail which gave it an alternative name of 'fork-tailed petrel'.

We spent a day on the headland of Dun which reminds me so much of Mykineshólmur in the Faroes. It too is separated from the main island by a very similar chasm - which hasn't been bridged - and it too has a large puffin colony.

I wandered among the stone *cleithan* above the village, and imagined them hanging with sides of mutton and gannets, or perhaps some of them held hay for the animals or peat for burning.

The St Kildans had to leave most of their sheep behind when they left the island, and these now run wild. Those that live around the village are used to people and are not too shy. They belong to the primitive Soay breed and are attractive animals (as sheep go!). They are as agile as goats on their spindly legs, and can be seen grazing on cliff ledges which you would swear were inaccessible to anything without wings.

Where crops once grew in the village, there is now a wilderness of grass and wildflowers, with yellow irises, lousewort and spotted orchis.

I once watched a television documentary about St Kilda, during which they interviewed some of the few people living who had been born and had spent their youth on the island. Most agreed that they had moments of nostalgia and longing to be back on the island, and one man, when pressed about why he admitted to such feelings, thought for a moment and then said 'It was chust a far better place. . .'

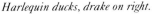

Harlequin ducks, drake on right.

7 ARCTIC ADVENTURE - SPITSBERGEN

The phone call came right out of the blue: would I like to take a small party up north to Spitsbergen? Trying not to let excitement show in my voice I said, 'Hold on while I check my diary' knowing fine that whatever was committed would have to be re-arranged!

Arctic fox still with some winter coat left.

It was all right, however. August is a fairly quiet month in Shetland apart from social functions like sailing regattas. Most of the summer breeding birds have either lost or won the battle for survival by then, common seal pups have been weaned and are now learning to fend for themselves. Early flowering plants such as marsh marigolds, spring squill and thrift are but a memory as the rich smell of cloves wafts across the fields from the stands of bog asphodel.

But in the Arctic, summer is just past its peak, with the pack ice as far north as it is likely to be, although in a month the first skin of new ice will tinkle and shimmer as it is broken up by the morning breeze.

The archipelago of Svalbard is Europe's most northerly land, lying only 900 kilometres from the North Pole and some 600 kilometres north of Tromsø in northern Norway. It would be reasonable to suppose that at this latitude the islands would be frozen in for most - if not all - of the year, and so they would, were it not for the Gulf Stream.

This great ocean current, with its origins in the warm waters of the Gulf of Mexico, streams north with many twists and meanderings, sending offshoots round the north of Britain and on up the Norwegian coast. By the time it reaches the coasts of West Spitsbergen, the largest of the Svalbard group, the current, although much reduced in strength, still has enough energy, when coupled with the summer sun, to warm the sea temperature enough to keep the ice at bay.

This means that for a few months in summer it is usually possible to sail right round West Spitsbergen; if the ship is not too large and is able to land passengers from suitable landing craft, this is the best possible way to explore Spitsbergen. And this was what we proposed to do, based on the Dutch ship 'Plancius', a sturdy forty metre long ex-pilot-boat which was well equipped for Arctic exploration with up to twenty-four passengers.

West Spitsbergen is roughly the size of Ireland. It is mountainous and glaciated with about sixty per cent of the land permanently covered in ice, and a coastline indented by many fiords. There are tundra slopes and river valleys where the soil supports enough plants and mosses to feed limited numbers of reindeer. Polar bears, especially mothers with cubs, tend to spend the summer on the islands, where they also graze on the vegetation. Most adult male bears spend their lives out on the pack ice, living mainly on seals.

West Spitsbergen is a cold and mountainous land with many permanent glaciers in the valleys and spectacular mountain and cliff scenery. The effects of erosion are clearly seen on this splendid section of sea-cliff, which lies on the south side of Isfjorden between the Norwegian coal-mining village of Longyearbyen and the Russian one at Barentsburg.

Seals and walrus live around the coasts, minke whales, belugas and other cetaceans are often seen, and of course there are the birds. Brünnich's guillemots, little auks, pink-footed geese and glaucous gulls share cliff habitats, while inland crags are tenanted by barnacle geese, black guillemots, snow buntings and even ivory gulls. Waders such as purple sandpipers, turnstones and a few grey phalarope share the tundra habitat.

All this, plus many 'new' Arctic flowers, The prospect was very exciting.

Spitsbergen was first mentioned in the old Icelandic annals of the year 1194, and was said to lie 'four days sailing from Langanes, at the northern end of the sea' They called it Svalbard, the 'cold coast'.

But strangely, nothing further was heard of the islands for several hundred years until the famous Dutch explorer Willem Barents rediscovered Svalbard in 1596. He had set out to try and find a passage to the Orient round the north of Asia in the hope that this would rid the merchant ships of the scourge of pirates who were terrorising the southern trade routes.

Instead, he discovered the archipelago of Svalbard, whose fiords were teeming with whales and walrus. This was such an important discovery that he sent his consort back to Holland to spread the good news while his ship continued alone. Alas,

Barents got no further than Novaya Zemlja, a large island in the Russian Arctic, about a thousand kilometres east of Svalbard. They became trapped in the ice. There was no escape and in the course of the following winter a number of the crew, including Barents himself, perished.

But news of the huge numbers of whales sparked off several expeditions, and the word spread. Before long English, French, Danish and Basque whale-hunters had all joined in the lucrative trade. Trouble flared as claims were disputed, and pitched battles were fought when warships were sent north to defend the claims of national whaling expeditions.

Inevitably, the stocks of whales became depleted, and by the middle of the eighteenth century the whaling at Svalbard (or, as it was called, the 'East Greenland Fishery') had ceased altogether. The operations then transferred to the west of Greenland, and at this stage many Shetlanders became involved as crew members on whaling ships, particularly those from Hull, Dundee and Peterhead. This continued until that fishery also finished around the turn of the present century.

Despite the harsh climate of Spitsbergen, several members of the gull family make it their summer home. The glaucous gull is a familiar bird around the town-ships near the coal-mining areas of Spitsbergen, scavenging as gulls do for anything edible round the village or raiding little auk colonies for eggs and young. It looks quite a lot like a (large) herring gull, but the main distinguishing features are the all-white primary wing-feathers. This bird was standing on the quay at Barentsburg.

In the early eighteenth century, Russian fur-trappers began to work in Svalbard, even overwintering in order to trap Arctic fox and polar bear, and to hunt walrus and seal. Towards the end of that century, Norwegian hunters also began to visit West Spitsbergen, where they, too, built huts and cabins. Many of these can still be seen to this day. These early settlers used to heat their cabins in winter with coal which they could gather from the mountain-sides, and this natural resource also came to the notice of entrepreneurs. Among them was an American, John Longyear, who set up a mining operation on the shores of Isfjorden.

Pomerine Skua.

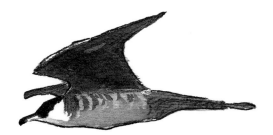

For hundreds of years Svalbard had been a 'no-man's-land,' but after the First World War Norway was granted sovereignty and the Norwegian flag was hoisted on 14th August 1925. According to the Svalbard treaty, the signatories retain the right to exploit any minerals. Today only Russia exercises that right and operates a coal mine at Barentsburg, a few kilometres down the fiord from Longyearbyen, the main Norwegian coal-mining area which the Store Norsk Spitzbergen Kulkompani bought from John Longyear.

In each of these mining 'towns' about two thousand people live and work. The houses are modern and living conditions are good, but most people would admit that tax concessions are the main incentives which encourage people to live and work in such extreme climatic conditions.

We landed at Tromsø, which is over three hundred kilometres north of the Arctic Circle, in a heatwave. Men in shirtsleeves and women in summer dresses were strolling around the airport and ice-cream vendors were doing a brisk trade. I met most of my party there because I had flown from Stavanger and they had arrived via Oslo, but we all boarded the plane bound for Longyearbyen with great anticipation.

Our first sight of the island was a sharp mountain peak jutting through the low cloud which unfortunately spoiled our view, but in minutes we were through the cloud and touching down on the long black runway which ran parallel to the shores of the fiord. With a minimum of formalities we were through customs and boarding a pick-up truck for the short drive to the quay where a dory was waiting to take us to 'Plancius'. It was only after we had settled in and had sorted out our luggage that we realised that although it was still broad daylight, our watches told us that it was nearly two o'clock in the morning! I had already seen a couple of ringed seals, several eider duck, many Arctic terns and kittiwakes and a few scruffy immature glaucous gulls before I crept into my bunk to sleep.

We weighed anchor next morning and sailed down the fiord on a calm sea. A minke whale (also known as the lesser rorqual) broke the surface and rolled over, showing its glistening black back with the small dorsal fin set well back. We watched its sedate progress for a while before turning into Grønfjorden and anchoring off Barentsburg.

Ashore we were greeted pleasantly by the Russians and invited to wander where we wished. The village is situated on a very steep hillside with steps leading up to the next row of houses. Well-dressed men and women were walking around, almost everyone wearing the ubiquitous fur hat and huge pictures of Lenin looked down from hoardings. I was more interested in the kittiwakes nesting on the window ledges, and spent some time photographing them.

Down on the dark grey beach there was a collection of glaucous gulls and a few purple sandpipers, and then to my delight a snow white ivory gull flew in and settled on the shingle, giving me the chance to stalk and photograph one of the world's rarer gulls. This is a true Arctic species, the only European breeding-ground being the ice-surrounded crags of Svalbard. It rarely wanders as far south as the British or northern European coasts in winter. It is often seen scavenging along the edge of the pack and regularly follows polar bears to feed on the remains of seal kills.

When we got out into the open sea beyond the fiord, we began to see more auks, mainly Brüinnich's guillemots and little auks, and a lot more fulmar flying around. Unlike the more southern fulmars I had been used to seeing, which are mainly white with grey backs, these northern birds were nearly all a dark smoky grey. This seems an odd reversal of the usual rule that Arctic animals are whiter, but otherwise they behaved as fulmar do in Shetland, appearing to spend much of their time flying and gliding over the sea.

The next day we spent the forenoon ashore at Smeerenburg looking at the remains of the old Dutch whaling-station, and setting our feet for the first time on the Spitsbergen tundra.

The first flowering plant I saw was a familiar one - the purple mountain saxifrage, *Saxafraga oppositifolia* to give it the scientific name. As many plants are called by different 'popular' names in different countries, using the scientific name pretentious as it might sound, is sometimes the only way to check on correct identification. Other saxifrages I identified at Smeerenburg were *nivalis, ceruna, rivularis* and the very common *cespitosa*, the tufted saxifrage.

A few reindeer were grazing on the sparse tundra. These Spitsbergen animals are smaller and stockier than those of Lappland. They were wary and wouldn't stay to be photographed.

We continued along the north coast of West Spitsbergen, with a detour to the little atoll of Moffen Island. Here we hoped to see walrus. We circled round the island, which is little more than a circular shingle bar with a lagoon in the middle. There was a red-throated diver with young on the lagoon, along with a flock of Brent geese and some eider duck, but no signs of the animal we were looking for.

We were beginning to see a few icebergs now, incredibly blue and in all kinds of weird shapes; we had another reminder of just how far north we were, when a biting breeze blew up and it started snowing.

We ran into the shelter of Murchison Fiord, which is on the west side of Nordaustlandet. This is the second largest of the Svalbard islands, and much of its 15,000 square kilometres is covered in permanent ice.

The snow was beginning to turn to rain next morning and, although the ground was white right to the shores, we all went ashore and walked for several hours. We saw little wildlife. The vegetation was covered in snow, and only a couple of Arctic and one pomarine skua flew past. Smaller than the great skua but a little larger than the Arctic, the most obvious features of the pomarine are the two central tail-feathers which are considerably longer than the rest. Unlike both Arctic and long-tailed skuas, which have pointed central feathers, those of the pomarine are spoon-shaped and are very obvious in adult birds. An ivory gull and an Arctic fox on the beach cheered us up, and we ate our pack lunch in the shelter of a deserted Swedish scientific station near the shore.

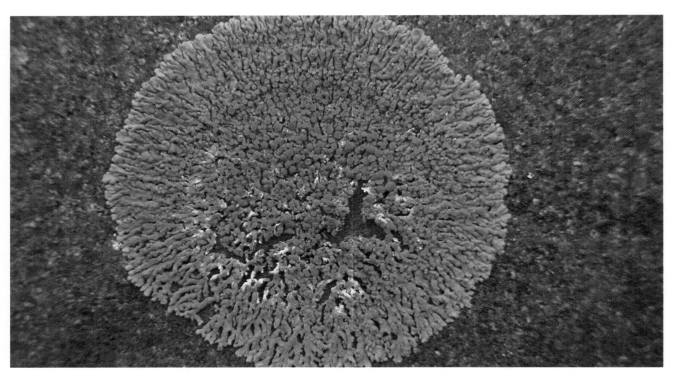

Much of Spitsbergen is barren of vegetation except in the river valleys and low ground near the coast where for a brief period in summer the ground may be carpeted with Arctic flowers. But even so it is not without colour, as many of the rocks are clad in lichens of different kinds. This glowing orb of orange lichen caught my eye and I marvelled again at the designs of nature.

After that the weather reverted to the normal Arctic summer: light winds and good visibility with often high cloud and the temperature well above freezing.

My photographic equipment was a bit limited by the fact that as a leader I was required to carry a heavy hunting rifle all the time we were ashore, just in case we met with a polar bear in a nasty mood. So far we hadn't seen a bear at all.

After only a short while ashore the next day at Vibebukta, we were recalled by the ship's hooter. The captain was becoming worried by the amount of ice setting into

The spectacular Saxifraga flagellaris *is called 'spider plant' and is one of the rarest Arctic saxifrages. Its curious red aerial roots make it look like a giant red spider.*

the bay and was anxious not to be trapped. The next few hours were worrying ones as we threaded our way between broken floe-ice, sometimes having to abort 'leads' and try others.

Bearded seals were hauled out on the ice-floes here and there and there were occasional puffins and guillemots in the bits of open water. Then someone cried 'Polar bear!' and sure enough, there was a large bear eating what appeared to be the remains of a seal.

It was too far away to make photography worthwhile, but through binoculars we could see that it was trying to cover the remains of its meal by pawing snow over it, and that a group of glaucous and ivory gulls were standing around, no doubt waiting in the hope of leftovers.

Polar bears are massive animals. Strong enough to whip a 150-kilogramme seal out of the water with one paw, able to swim many kilometres in freezing seas and quite

Of the thirty-four known species of seals in the world the great majority are found in the colder waters near the poles. In Spitsbergen the common species are the small ringed seal and the bearded seal. The one in the photograph is a young female bearded seal and I took the picture not in Spitsbergen, but in Shetland! Occasionally these animals wander away from their normal home.

above: *The charismatic ivory gull is a rare visitor to the British coasts and is certain to excite birdwatchers whenever it pays a visit. We were thrilled to find a small breeding colony high up on an island crag on Noraustlandet, the easternmost island in the Svalbard group.*

right:
This young polar bear (probably aged about eighteen months) attached itself to a party of scientists living in an old trappers' cabin on Edgeøya, and when we got there (after the scientists had departed) the bear came up looking for pack lunches!

capable of climbing up almost vertical ice-faces, they represent one of nature's supreme examples of adaptation to an inhospitable environment.

Adult males are nomadic, wandering all round the polar ice cap and living mainly off seals. Females choose to give birth to their one or two young in dens dug into the snow-drifts on mountainsides of places such as the Svalbard Islands, and often stay on the islands during the Arctic summer until the cubs are old enough to fend for themselves.

Eventually - and with some relief - we were out into open water and setting course for the other two large islands in the group, Barentsøvya and Edgeøya. We spent a day ashore on Barentsøya where the Dutch party went off inland on their own and met up with a polar bear with two cubs, which ran off when they saw the party. We stayed mainly near the shore and saw ringed seals and a nice flock of Brent geese. Later in the evening, as we sailed south along the coast several more polar bears were spotted on the mountain-sides.

We were trying to find a way through the pack ice in Hinlopen Strait when we spotted a large male polar bear eating the remains of a seal on the ice. Although too far away for a good photograph, we all clicked away in hope, while the captain concentrated on getting his ship out of a tricky situation.

Next day we went ashore near Kapp Lee on Edgeøya, and had a long walk up through Rosenbergdalen, a fine valley which was much more vegetated than any we had so far seen. There was extensive ground cover of polar willows, yellow and white whitlow-grass, scurvy grass and many others. We had lunch on the side of the valley as a polar bear lay sleeping opposite us on the other side! Farther down the coast we saw a huge kittiwake colony on an inland cliff and went to investigate. Below the nesting area the slopes were rich with vegetation, enriched by bird-droppings, and we were climbing up the slope when we became aware that a polar bear with a big cub was 'grazing' on the slope.

She spotted us at the same time and after a long look, took her offspring and ambled away along the side of the mountain. The pair then lay down and went to sleep!

We climbed as near to the base of the cliff as possible, and startled an Arctic fox which trotted off unhurriedly. There was a small, partly hidden gully at the base of the cliff and there, grazing on the scurvy grass, was yet another bear. It was less than a hundred metres away, and gave us a long hard look as we stood there. Then it appeared to decide we weren't a threat - or a source of food - and carried on munching the vegetation.

We were to have an even closer encounter with a bear before we left Edgeøya, when we went ashore at the south end of the island at Andrée Tangen. It was one of those typical Arctic mornings, with the sun shining through a veil of sea-mist which limited visibility at sea level to a hundred metres or so. 'Plancius' was anchored some way offshore because of shallow water and reefs, so when the first party went off in the inflatable, we could see no land at all and had to steer by compass. As the dim outline of a beach was beginning to show, three huge heads broke the surface ahead of us and we nearly ran into three walrus.

They were huge animals, with tusks about sixty centimetres long and they seemed as curious about us as we were excited to see them. Cameras were hurriedly produced, which was no easy matter as we were squeezed in a very small boat, and everyone was in everyone else's way as we tried to take photographs. One particularly bold animal came so close that we thought he was going to hook his tusks over the edge of our inflatable. This could have had unfortunate consequences, so we started up the motor and went on towards the beach. The walrus followed us in to the shallows, and we hurriedly jumped out on to the shore to get better pictures.

I was just pressing the camera shutter when someone yelled 'Polar bear!' and there, about twenty metres away on the head of the beach, was a bear standing watching us.

Survival instincts took precedence, and I was all thumbs as I disentangled camera, binocular, rucksack and rifle straps from round my neck. By the time I was ready (if

Hunting pressures have sadly depleted the stocks of walrus round the Spitsbergen area, though with protection there are signs of a slow increase. We saw only three in our circumnavigation. They were feeding in relatively shallow water near the island of Edgeøya. Walruses are large animals: an adult male can be three metres in length and weigh 1200 kg.

Occasional wanderers have turned up as far south as the southern North Sea, and Shetland has had several sightings.

it became necessary) to defend the party, the bear had got fed up waiting, had sat down on its backside and was yawning. It was at that point we realised it wasn't a very large bear. In fact it was quite a small bear. It was probably the effect of the fog that had made it seem huge at first.

We heard the story of the bear later. A couple of scientists had been working on Edgeøya for most of the summer, and this young bear had appeared near the old trapper's hut they were staying in (which was near the beach where we had landed). It was suffering from a bad wound on its hip, and it had either lost or been abandoned by its mother. The scientists fed the little bear as best they could, and the wound healed up, but the cub just stayed around the hut. The men had been gone several weeks, and when we appeared on the beach, the bear was probably expecting us to produce food.

Each of us had a pack lunch in our bag and someone tentatively offered the bear a ham sandwich. We might have known what would happen! Everyone went hungry that day, because the little polar bear scoffed every pack lunch we had. I hope it helped a little, because the chances of it surviving the winter were probably slim.

Well, the two weeks were drawing to a close and we rounded the point of Sørkapp (South Cape) and headed back towards Longyearbyen. We marvelled again at the scenery of West Spitsbergen, its sharply tipped mountains of dark rock, the glacier-filled valleys between and the tiny strips of life-giving vegetation which made it possible for some birds and animals to exist.

I couldn't help wondering for how much longer the thousands of sea-birds nesting on the cliffs, the seals and the whales would find abundant supplies of food in the seas of the Arctic. Industrial fishing has already decimated stocks of capelin, the small fish which, like the sand-eel in Shetland waters, is the principal food for many birds and animals.

Surely sense will prevail before it is too late - we can only hope. . .

8 AUTUMN DAYS

Twite.

For me, the first equinoctial gales - usually in late September - signal the start of autumn. But that is because so much of my summer activity revolves around boats and the sea - other people may well have different 'season indicators'.

During the summer months I can usually get away with leaving my boat conveniently tied up to the pier, but only if I am at home to keep an eye on the weather: in Shetland, even in summer, a gale can blow up from the south east, causing a swell to set into the voe. This can result in boats 'surging' and breaking mooring 'bitts' or even mooring-ropes.

So, winter moorings have to be overhauled, making sure that the chain hasn't become too worn and that shackles are secure. When a good-going winter gale sets in, a week or more may pass without a break in the weather to allow the boat to be checked and any rain water to be pumped out.

Crofters and farmers see things differently, of course. Harvesting methods have changed over the years and even on small crofts there is mechanisation. Hand-cutting of hay by scythe is almost a thing of the past, as people either have their own tractor-driven machines or can hire someone to do the job.

For several reasons (some of them government imposed), fewer cattle are now kept on the crofts in Shetland, and the accent is more on sheep-rearing. This means that fewer cereal crops (such as oats) are grown and more land is put down to grass. This has had its effect on some birds: the fields which used to be sown with oats meant stubble in autumn and winter which held large quantities of seeds.

It wasn't only the seeds of oats; the cornfields usually contained quantities of weeds like chickweed, spurrey and charlock and it was on all these that the skylarks, twite and rock doves fattened up for the coming winter. This food was also an invaluable help to passage migrants such as the finches and buntings, helping them put on a few extra grammes of fat to carry them through the next leg of their long journey to winter quarters.

Due to the availability of government grants, crofters can now fence off their allocation of the common grazings, and, with applications of limestone and fertiliser, can convert heather-covered hillsides to grass fields which can 'carry' more sheep in the same area of ground. This suits some birds and spoils things for others.

Greylag and pink-footed geese, which breed in Iceland, spend the winter feeding on the grassland and winter wheat-fields of the big fertile farms of eastern Scotland. It often happens that while on their southward migration in autumn, they get forced off course by westerly gales, at times arriving in Shetland in large numbers. Not finding suitable feeding they use the islands only to rest briefly and re-orientate, before setting a new course for their chosen destination.

But in recent years some greylag geese have begun to stay over the winter, finding the large re-seeded fields to their liking. Not only that, but a few pairs have stayed

overleaf: *With its clear cool air, Shetland can produce spectacular sunsets on occasion, and if you can include cliffs or seascape in the picture it helps evokes memories. It was the cloud formations which caught my eye on this occasion and suggested a telephoto shot. The Ramna Stacks on the horizon are an RSPB reserve and house about 10,000 sea-birds in the summer.*

Rosefinch in autumn.

on to breed, and in certain areas half a dozen or more broods of young can be seen on the new grassland.

An autumn migrant to Shetland, is the waxwing. They breed in the forests of northern Scandinavia and Siberia and live on berries and fruit.

On the other hand the loss of heather has meant a contraction of the breeding-grounds for birds like golden plover, dunlin, and perhaps whimbrel, although the post-breeding flocks of these species seem to favour the re-seeded grassland. Some 'improvements' to the grazing have meant the draining of small marshes and this, of course, can have a serious effect on birds like snipe and redshank.

The arrival in spring of our breeding birds and migrants is usually well documented: the first singing skylark and blackbird, the arrival of wheatear, bonxie and whimbrel often rate a mention on local news broadcasts or in weekly newspapers. But only those people who are serious enough about birds to keep daily diaries will have recorded the last dates birds were seen before they departed to their winter quarters.

In Shetland the situation is a bit confused by the migration of birds from other, usually more northerly areas. Sometimes there is a distinct gap between our birds leaving and others passing through. Arctic terns may disappear during August and then reappear after a week or two.

To get proof that these are not 'our' birds is not easy, but is illustrated by an incident which happened a few years ago.

On a shingle spit which connects a tiny island to the shores of Mainland, a tern colony became established every summer, and the local crofter would stop taking his tractor over to the island during the time the birds were nesting. In late August, after

The oil rigs and production platforms which are situated out in the North Sea provide 'emergency accommodation' for exhausted migrants during their journey across the inhospitable ocean. I photographed this blue-tit on Ninian Central platform - a far cry from the usual suburban garden!

There are a number of kinds of cetaceans (whales and dolphins) seen from time to time in the waters around Shetland. The smallest is the common porpoise, or neesick, as we call it.
It is a rather independent little beast, not given to sporting with boats like some of the bigger dolphins.

the terns had fledged, he went over one evening to do some work on the island, and on the way back in the dusk he disturbed a party of terns which were roosting on the beach, one of which flew into the tractor and was killed. He picked up the bird and noticed it had a ring on its leg, so he wrote down the number and passed the information on to me. In due course the details of the recovery filtered back and we learned that the tern had been ringed as a fledgling in a colony in southern Sweden only a couple of weeks earlier.

Birds which have significantly different plumage in different areas are a bit easier. The post-breeding flocks of golden plover sometimes have the odd individual still in summer dress, with the much darker 'shirt-front' suggesting an Icelandic origin.

We keep a check on the Shetland eider population by counting the males when they gather into moult flocks at traditional sites. They lose their flight feathers in August and are flightless until the new feathers grow back.

In other birds a size difference is the giveaway: the wheatear is a summer visitor to Shetland, generally leaving in August or September, and it is only when birds of the race which breeds in Greenland, which are distinctly bigger, are seen that we know strangers are passing through.

Another phenomenon of late summer and autumn is the arrival of so-called 'irruptive' species. These are birds, generally of Scandinavian woodland origin, which have bred in large numbers and then presumably find themselves short of food. Typical of these is the crossbill, a bird of the pine forests, which every few years arrives in Shetland in flocks.

1990 was such a year, when successive waves of these birds made their appearance from late July until well through September. In the absence of their normal woodland habitat, they could be found in all sorts of unlikely places. I saw parties feeding on the seed-heads of thrift in the middle of a gannet colony, on the seeds of rushes out on the windswept moors, and in my own garden where they quickly cleaned up the remaining rowan berries. With their plumage of mixed reds and greens, crossbills are noticeable birds. They are normally tame and approachable, allowing a look at the large beak with the crossed-over tips to the mandibles which gives the bird its name.

An even more startling species to arrive in numbers to Shetland is the great spotted woodpecker. Again late August or early September is the likely time for these beautiful woodland birds to appear. But they must find Shetland pretty inhospitable, with no trees to support the grubs which is their normal diet.

They can often be seen climbing up creosoted telegraph-poles in a vain search for food. In fact, I was told of an occasion when a power-pole had to be replaced because a woodpecker had dug a hole 'you could hide a beer can in', as my informant said!

The third, and perhaps the most beautiful, of the 'irruptive' species is the waxwing. From their breeding grounds in northern Scandinavia - or even Siberia - they arrive in Shetland in October or November. They live mainly on berries and fruit, so they tend to home in on people's gardens. Being another approachable bird,

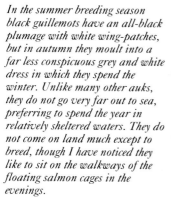

In the summer breeding season black guillemots have an all-black plumage with white wing-patches, but in autumn they moult into a far less conspicuous grey and white dress in which they spend the winter. Unlike many other auks, they do not go very far out to sea, preferring to spend the year in relatively sheltered waters. They do not come on land much except to breed, though I have noticed they like to sit on the walkways of the floating salmon cages in the evenings.

and very distinctive in their cinnamon-coloured plumage, with a crest on their head and bright red 'waxy' tips to the secondary wing feathers, they do tend to get noticed and reported.

The sad fact is that many of these 'irruptive' birds spend their last days in the islands, because if they do not move on immediately while they still have the strength, the more time they spend searching for what isn't there, the less chance there is of their being able to make another long sea crossing.

The autumn passage of birds through Shetland tends to be more noticeable than in spring, and there are several reasons for this: there are many more birds on the move because the migrating flocks include all the young birds raised during the summer. The birds tend to stay in Shetland longer because there is much more food available in the form of seeds and insects at the end of the summer, than at the end of the winter. Depression fronts tend to occur more frequently, causing the birds to use Shetland as a 'filling station' until the storm blows over.

No one can ever know the fatality rate, the numbers of young inexperienced birds

Although it is really a sea-bird, the red-throated diver has become so specialised that it can scarcely walk and its unable to get airborne from the ground. So it nests close to the edges of little pools on the moorland where it can slip off its nest into the water and use that as a runway. Young, inexperienced birds sometimes try to fly before they are quite ready, and may crash-land on the moors. They may then stagger to the nearest stream and follow that to the sea. The bird in the photograph was doing just that.

who are tempted to take on the flight across the North Sea, but who never make it. It is no wonder that so many of the small northern birds have to raise large broods of young, just to maintain the status quo of the population. 'Any port in a storm' is an often-quoted truism, and for migrant birds this is certainly the case.

After the hectic activity of summer, I look forward to doing more relaxed boating and fishing trips in early autumn. One of our regular activities in August or early in September is the annual eider duck monitoring count. Ever since the oil companies came to Shetland they, along with the local authority, have supported regular sea-bird monitoring programmes, with a full-time independent biologist to run them. In the event of an oil spill, our resident eider population would be high on the list of vulnerable species, and warrants a special effort to assess and monitor the Shetland population.

The larger of the two kinds of seal which breed in Shetland, grey seals have a different way of doing things. The common seals have their pups in June when the weather is fine, but the greys wait until autumn and the equinoctial gales before they haul out on to beaches below the high cliffs. When the pups are born they are covered in white fur, but they moult into the beautiful coat seen in the picture before going off to sea.

During flightless stage of their summer moult, eider drakes all gather at 'traditional' sites in flocks sometimes over a thousand strong, and this is the best time to get an accurate estimate of the size of the population.

One of the problems is that these moult-sites are usually as far from man's activities as possible, often near remote skerries, headlands or small uninhabited islands, and this necessitates the use of a boat in most cases. So, whenever the weather is suitable during the critical period, a phone call from Martin will put me on the alert.

The call came at seven thirty in the morning. Martin reported that the Met. Office forecast was that the winds would be light until late afternoon, then would increase to force five by dusk. We could do it if we didn't hang about. I looked at the time. 'See you at Vidlin about ten thirty', I said.

Taking a pint of milk from the fridge, and a few slices of fresh bread, I lost no time in getting 'Starna' under way. As soon as I was clear of the entrance to the voe, I let the boat steer herself while I put the kettle on for a cuppa after a modest breakfast of bread and cheese. I switched the VHF radio on and listened to the banter of the salmon boys going out to 'feed their flocks'. I also switched on the echo-sounder and adjusted it to 'bleep' if we passed over any fish - such are the benefits of modern technology!

Just over two hours later I nosed into the pier at Vidlin and Martin and Lucy jumped on board. Lucy was involved in a study of cetaceans and had come along in the hope of seeing at least some porpoises.

We set a course for Out Skerries in good visibility and fairly calm seas. There were few birds, only small groups of tysties feeding near the shore, the newly fledged youngsters in grey and white plumage, and the adults already moulting into their winter shades of grey.

Out in the open firth a few gannets were flying about, watching for any fish movement and occasionally making what seemed like exploratory dives. If they did catch anything they had swallowed it before surfacing.

Near Muckla Skerry there was a bit more action: groups of porpoises were puffing their way along. This pleased Lucy, who plotted their position and course.

We passed close by the islet, disturbing a number of grey seals basking on the dark rocks and putting a party of shags to flight. A number of common guillemots were feeding in the tidal streams which run strongly here.

Checking out Litla Skerry and the Vongs (fangs) - two isolated groups of rocks west of Out Skerries, where small groups of eider had been known to shelter - without finding any eider, we then went north around the main island, getting occasional glimpses of houses through the narrow entrances to the harbour. For the Out Skerries comprise a group of three little islands which are conveniently arranged to form a perfect natural harbour. This provides shelter for a small fishing fleet, which supports a population of nearly a hundred people. Without a harbour, the islands would probably not be inhabited at all, as the land area is only about 250 hectares.

Of the many birds which pass through Shetland in autumn, not all are in the plumage depicted in the bird books. When a neighbour reported an unusual bird in his garden and I went to check it out, I stared in disbelief! From various clues I eventually worked out what it was. Can you? You will find the answer somewhere in the text.

When most crofters kept a few cows and cultivated oats and hay for winter feeding, the stubble fields provided rich pickings for many birds, either during their stop-over on migration or for the local birds - especially the crop of young birds all anxious to put on the maximum of fat as a reserve against the lean days of winter.

Shetland rock doves are more important than many people realise because they are the last remnants of the pure ancestral stock from which all the town pigeons of the world have developed. They breed as they have always done, in the sea caves and crevices in the cliffs, and in the winter they make regular forays to the croft stackyards to feed on the stocks of oats - as the birds in the photographs are doing.

We found the eider flock at the back of Bound Skerry, on which the lighthouse stands. There were several hundred birds and, because we had rounded a corner and surprised them, they panicked and went rushing off in a tight bunch, making an accurate count impossible. We stopped the boat and drifted for a while, and the birds relaxed and moved back towards Bound Skerry the rock in a long line - which did the trick!

We found a few more smaller parties near the Benelips and Filla, two small grass-topped islets which form the south-western extremity of Out Skerries. Then, confident that we hadn't missed many, we set course for the larger island of Whalsay.

The kettle went on for a lunchtime brew-up before we tackled the group of small, uninhabited islands which lie west of Whalsay: Nacka Skerry, Nista, Mooa, Isbister Holm (the only place in Shetland where sea-aster grows), East Linga and Grif Skerry. All are small islets only a few thousand square metres in extent, which support a few Shetland sheep, a sizable common seal population and a few birds.

We had to circle all the islands in case we missed the eider. When they are in moult they often sit ashore on the rocks, when their dark brown plumage blends in with the dark rocks. Most of the ducks were at Grif Skerry as we expected and, after counts and recounts, we moved on.

The wind had freshened by this time and was causing some choppy waves, so we pressed on to try and finish the circuit planned before counting became impossible.

The spaced out and rather dangerous reefs called the Fladdacaps and the Billians

all hold small groups of moulting eider and all were checked and counted until finally, after rounding the Hoo Stack, we headed for home, running before the rising wind.

Noticing some birds feeding near the Inner Voder, we made a detour and were delighted to find a party of Manx shearwaters. This bird nests in very small numbers in Shetland, although because of its nocturnal habits and the difficulties of examining the steep, grassy cliff-slopes in which it digs out its burrows, I am sure not all the colonies have been located. Perhaps this flock were nesting on the grassy top of Hoo Stack, who knows?

Pallas' warbler.

After dropping Martin and Lucy off at Vidlin, I set off for home. It was dark and the sea was rising rapidly as I came up the firth, keeping the bows in the direction of the flashing lighthouse on the White Hill of Vatster. But the wind was behind me and each wave picked up the boat and surged her ahead, so that I tied up at the pier some fifteen hours after I had left, a little tired but satisfied that another small gap in our knowledge of birds had been filled.

October is the month of 'all change' in Shetland. Out go the small birds: no longer does the song of the skylark, the flirting wheatears, or the parachuting meadow pipits greet us as we walk the moors. The dive-bombing skuas, the screaming terns, the lovely trilling whimbrel and dunlin and the wailing divers, all are silent and will be seen and heard no more until spring arrives to warm the earth and banish the snows of winter.

But even though some of the birds we look on as 'ours' leave for more hospitable climes before the onset of winter, there are others to whom the Shetland climate is perfectly acceptable. The stately whooper swans fly in from Iceland in late September or October, the timing probably depending on how soon the first winter frosts set in up north.

The first parties of long-tailed ducks will arrive early in October, and glaucous gulls in first-winter plumage will join our resident herring and black-backed gulls to forage along the shores or scrounge a living at the salmon farms.

The last of the shore birds will probably have arrived by this time. Turnstones and purple sandpipers will join the redshanks and ringed plovers which are probably resident.

October often sees the biggest passage of Scandinavian migrants of the year. Fieldfares, redwing and song thrush sometimes flood the islands in thousands, and flocks are scanned eagerly in the hope of finding one of the rarer Siberian thrushes such as black-throated or White's. It is impossible for us to know exactly what circumstances combine to bring these extreme rarities to the islands: after breeding in north-eastern Siberia, they should be on their way to Manchuria for the winter. But almost every year one or more of these Siberian thrushes or warblers turn up to add a bit of icing to the bird-watching cake!

Masses of willow warblers, chiff-chaffs, blackcaps, whitethroats and sometimes yellow-browed or Pallas's warblers will set the pulses racing, and the flocks of chaffinch and brambling will be painstakingly examined in the hope of finding perhaps a little bunting, rustic bunting or Arctic redpoll.

It never ceases to amaze me how nature has endowed these tiny bodies with the instincts, the strength and endurance to undertake such fantastic journeys every year of their lives.

Redwings and fieldfares overhead.

Autumn is merging into winter. When the clocks go back in late October it will be dark by five o'clock in the afternoon. The equinoctial gales make a couple of attempts to scare us, but like an old Shetland pony we turn our backs to the wind and stick it out. The only casualties I hear of are a couple of pleasure boats which dragged their moorings and were damaged on the shore. We have long accepted the principle that 'if you live by the river you must make friends with the crocodile' and prepare for the certainty that sooner or later winds of hurricane force will hit the islands. At the height of the gale I go down to the pier to see how our local boats are doing, but all the anchors appear to be holding firm.

The wind is probably gusting to sixty or seventy knots with spindrift flying everywhere, yet on the pier a group of herring gulls are standing with their feet flat on the concrete and *not* being blown away. How do they do it?

The answer must be that the bird is designed by nature for this medium in the same way that dolphins are designed for life beneath the sea. Dolphins (and many other sea creatures) can, by muscular power and their own dynamic shape, attain speeds in water which man cannot yet emulate without using excessive amounts of power. And so the gulls can absorb or accommodate the pressures of the wind, standing apparently unconcerned in gusts which are tossing around 180-litre oil drums like playthings.

Once the gales have blown themselves out and the depressions have 'filled' or moved away, we usually get a spell of settled weather when things return to normal. The few days of settled weather allow me to spend some hours fishing offshore for ling and tusk which, as well as providing me with relaxation and sport, is satisfyingly justified in my own mind because it is providing food for the family during the winter to come. Although deep-freezing has revolutionised the way food is preserved, with some kinds of fish I still prefer the old method of salting and sun drying.

It was Isaak Walton who wisely said. 'There is more to fishing than just to fish' and how right he was. Drifting offshore with the wind and tide is a splendid way to get a close look at sea-birds, because they have come to accept fishing-boats as a source of food rather than a potential danger. This applies mainly to the opportunist feeders like gulls, fulmars, skuas and to some extent gannets. The auks, while they do not appear to recognise man as a benefactor, certainly are aware of the signals given by other birds. So if the gulls and others are relaxed and 'happy', the auks in turn will behave more naturally towards fishing-boats.

To some extent this applies also to whales and dolphins: some, such as white-sided and white-beaked dolphins, appear to enjoy a boat going at speed and will actively approach and 'bow-ride' for a time. But many species appear not to like the sound of a motor or a throbbing propeller. Perhaps it interferes with their own communicating system.

Lesser rorqual, pilot whales, Risso's dolphins, killer whales and porpoises are all likely to be met with in Shetland waters and most of my close encounters have been while I have been drifting with the motor stopped. The lesser rorqual (or minke, as it is called in Norway) is the largest of the cetaceans likely to be met with in inshore water around Shetland. It is one of the 'true' whales in that its mouth is furnished with plates of baleen (whalebone) through which it filters the water from the shoaling small fish on which it feeds. Unfortunately, with the decline of the bigger whales like the blue whale, right whale and others in the north Atlantic due to hunting pressures, attention turned to the smaller minke whale with the result that it too is becoming scarcer.

Killer whales and pilot whales belong to the group known as 'toothed whales' (and are related to the dolphins) and both are seen from time to time around Shetland. Killer whales are up to ten metres in length and can easily be identified by their black and white colour and the high dorsal fin of the males. They usually go round in family groups, and while they probably feed mainly on fish, they are able and willing to kill a seal if they find one.

Pilot whales are called 'caa'ing whales' in Shetland from the way their friendly and peaceable nature makes them easy to 'caa' or herd into shallow water. In the old days in Shetland (and still today in Faroe) this meant the animals could be driven on to a beach and killed.

It was on a fishing expedition in late autumn a year or two ago that we were visited by a number of pomarine skuas, no doubt birds from northern Siberia which were making their way towards wintering quarters in the south Atlantic. There had been severe westerly gales a few days before, and these skuas had probably been displaced off their normal migration routes by the storm.

They were obviously attracted to the boat by the number of 'gulls-in-waiting', and at one time there were fourteen of these handsome pirates flying around. Fortunately I had taken my camera-bag with me, so fishing was abandoned for a while as I attempted to take pictures of moving birds from a moving boat!

If I have been fishing to the north of Fetlar, I sometimes take the 'inner route' back, a rather tortuous passage through the reefs and islets where navigation has to be pretty precise to avoid hitting hidden rocks. I am not sure if any time is saved by taking this route, but it is much more interesting.

The area has a large common seal population, and there are always lots of them lying on the rocks or swimming in the sea. It is the main breeding place in the area and I often take visitors there in mid-June, when the pups are being born. Since hunting was stopped about twenty years ago, the behaviour of the seals has changed dramatically. No longer do they panic at the sound of a boat engine, and slap their drowsy pups awake to be hustled into the comparative safety of the sea. If they recognise the boat as 'friendly' and if it isn't rushing around at high speed, they will allow you to get close enough to take photographs.

Arctic redpolls.

Otters are also quite numerous in this area, and last season I had the pleasure of getting to know the habits of one particular animal. The reason I could recognise this individual with certainty was because of the exceptional colour of its coat. Most otters are dark brown with varying shades of paler brown on the throat and neck. This makes them very difficult to spot among the rocks, and especially among the brown seaweed. But this animal - which I nicknamed 'Ginger' - is fawn or biscuit-coloured all over.

Part of the inner route takes us through a narrow gap between a promontory of Fetlar called the Ness of Urie, and a small skerry which has a patch of grass on top. The gap between the two, although only a few metres wide, is deep enough for my boat to pass through at any state of tide.

Bluethroat on autumn migration.

I was negotiating this narrow gap one day early in the summer when my eye was caught by a patch of fawn colour among the green grassy top of the skerry. Through binoculars I could tell that it was part of an animal, and I could see it gently moving as it breathed. I stopped the boat and drifted as near as I dared. The otter either heard me or got my scent, because it suddenly looked up, then stood up and moved out of sight round the other side of the rock. It was an otter such as I had never seen before, with this all-over fawn coat.

There have been occasional sightings of albino or part albino otters in Shetland and, because this was a big animal and looked a bit 'grizzled' round the muzzle, I thought it was probably a very old dog otter. Next time I passed that way I kept a look-out, and sure enough, there it was, sleeping in the same 'couch' on the skerry.

In my spare time I was taking boat parties out from Mid Yell, and I 'used' that animal all summer, rarely failing to find it. But one day in late summer, when I was pointing the otter out to my passengers, and as usual it got up to move out of sight, I saw to my surprise that it was followed by two cubs! One was the normal otter colour but the other had fawn-coloured fur like its mother. I mentioned this to a Fetlar man who used to hunt otters for their pelts, as many crofters did and he could tell me that there had been pale-coated otters in that area for at least fifty years.

The sea temperature in Shetland never gets much above ten degrees Celsius even in summer, which doesn't encourage prolonged immersion without the protection of a wet-suit. But I am due to take a trip to the Indian Ocean shortly where I hope to go swimming in a warmer sea!

The mystery bird is an immature rose-coloured starling which hails from eastern Europe and is a vagrant to Britain.

Blackcap warbler.

9 SEYCHELLES - A TROPICAL PARADISE

The Indian mynah is an adaptable species, like all members of the starling tribe to which it belongs, and was introduced into the Seychelles sometime in the eighteenth century. It is noisy and extrovert, happy to make full use of man's activities. I get the strong impression that the mynah is - in bird terms - pretty clever at manipulating circumstances to its own advantage!

Only a few weeks after returning from playing with polar bears in Spitsbergen, I was soaking up the sun in the Seychelles. I knew something about the bird life of the islands, having read articles about the rare and endangered Seychelles kestrel and magpie robin, but it was a chance encounter in - of all places - the Falkland Islands, that inspired my partner in Island Holidays to seek out more information. Meeting Seychelles tourist reps at a Travel Trade Fair clinched it and arrangements were made for us to join a small group of people on an exploratory trip in October 1989.

So instead of thermal underwear and thick socks, I was packing sandals, shorts and summer shirts for the trip to the tropics.

The Seychelles lie in the middle of the Indian Ocean, just a few degrees south of the equator. Their slogan says 'unique by a thousand miles' and indeed they are around a thousand miles (1600 kilometres) from the coast of Africa. India to the north is much further away and their nearest neighbour of any size is Madagascar, which lies some 1200 kilometres away to the south west.

My first impression was of oppressive heat, but then I have spent my life mainly on the cool side of temperate. But it was only somewhere about thirty degrees Celsius and after a few days I had become accustomed to the change in temperature.

I also found the birdwatching a bit frustrating at first - there was so much vegetation, and so many places for birds to hide. Fortunately most birds were not shy, in fact many were ridiculously tame.

Wedge-tailed and Audubon's shearwaters.

The most noticeable bird was the Indian mynah. Bold and extrovert characters, they would sit on the bedroom balcony and shout raucously at each other, but they really are quite handsome birds.

Everywhere there was luxuriant vegetation. Hibiscus, frangipani, bougainvillaea and the glorious colours of the flame tree were a visual feast and a challenge for the camera which I felt unable to cope with at first. Coconut palms, mangroves and many unidentified trees confused me considerably, I who had been used to nothing taller than a stunted elder bush in a croft garden!

The harbour at Victoria was more to my liking, for here were extensive areas of tidal sands, all dotted with busily feeding waders. I was now in more familiar territory. Greenshank were dashing about nervously in the shallows, as greenshanks do, small parties of elegant curlew sandpipers were busily feeding by probing the sand, and grey plovers were standing about watching for any small movements. A whimbrel got up with its familiar tittering whistle and flew off across the sand-flats.

Most of these birds would have bred in the northern parts of Siberia, travelling thousands of kilometres to find a place in the Seychelles where they would be assured of a supply of suitable food.

Some of the waders were unfamiliar to me. One which looked like a ringed plover but with a brown tinge to its less contrasty plumage turned out to be greater sand plover, which breeds on the desert plains of Mongolia. Without recourse to books I recognised terek sandpiper with its long, slightly upturned bill and yellow legs. Although I hadn't come across this Siberian wader before, it does turn up in Shetland occasionally.

Many of these birds were feeding on tiny crabs with which the sands were teeming. I watched many abortive attempts to catch them, because these tiny crustaceans could sprint with amazing speed back to their burrows in the sand if they felt threatened.

Birds on the shore in the Seychelles. Crab plover, lesser crested tern, whimbrel, curlew sandpiper, mynah, cattle egret.

Dealing with the larger crabs was that outstanding bird, the crab plover. Almost a big as an oystercatcher, it is all white with black on the wings and back. It has a large black beak and long grey legs. It is only known to breed in the Gulf area, where it digs out burrows in the sand and, as its name suggests, it feeds almost exclusively on crabs.

It was not only waders that made use of the sand: green-backed herons, cattle egrets and a solitary grey heron were also busily feeding, and a distant party of little terns on a sand spit were probably the race called Saunders's tern, judging by the amount of dark on the wing-tips when they flew off. The little tern, as its name suggests, is one of the smallest of the tern tribe with about eight sub-species ranging widely over both hemispheres. Taxonomists are not yet in full agreement as to whether the bird most likely to be seen in the Seychelles rates as a full species. But some think it does and have named it Saunders's tern. To me the small group of birds on the sand-spit looked just like little terns, but it is a bird I have never seen in Shetland, so I am not familiar with it.

We were given a 'courtesy trip' round the periphery of the island of Mahe, which included a superb lunch at a seafood restaurant. It wasn't a 'birdy' trip, but nevertheless a few more species were ticked off. The little dark Seychelles sunbird was flitting about, sipping nectar from the many blossoms. White terns and tropic birds occasionally flew above the canopy of trees, and in the evening what looked like a flock of ravens soaring high above the hills turned out to be fruit-bats or 'flying foxes'.

The road round the island offers some spectacular vistas. Vast stretches of white sandy beaches, most of them empty of people, fringed by coconut palms and mangroves. Tempting little offshore islands, washed by warm blue seas - it seemed almost too good to be true!

Our next call was to Fregate Island, a twenty-minute flight in an 'Islander' eight-seater aircraft. As we taxied to a halt on the coastal grassy runway, we disturbed parties of curlew, sandpipers and grey plover. On going back to the airstrip later I found several Pacific golden plover with the greys. They are slimmer-looking birds than our own Eurasian plovers, and with darker underwings. They also have their breeding-grounds along the northern Siberian tundra belt beyond the treeline, illustrating again the fantastic migrations undertaken by these birds.

Accommodation on Fregate was in chalets thatched with palm leaves and situated on the top of the beach so that at high tide you could almost jump into the sea from your window. The central reception and dining area was under the shelter of a huge 'banyan' tree whose aerial roots hung back down to the ground like fronds. Near the entrance of the open-plan dining area was a large bird-table, and we saw the reason for that when meal-time came.

Just before guests sat down, one of the staff went out with a bucket of rice and scraps and was immediately mobbed by flocks of birds. This gave everyone a chance to have their meal without the attention of the doves and fodies, who would otherwise steal food from your table - or even off the plate in front of you. If you got up to fetch another cup of tea or coffee, you were liable to find that your plate had been cleaned out while you had been away.

Any crumbs which fell off the table were pounced on by big bronze lizards - skinks. Meal-times were never dull!

I have known turnstones all my life as common winter visitors to the coastal areas of Britain, and I have seen them on their breeding-grounds in Lappland and in Spitsbergen, but I hadn't really expected to find that they were 'bird-table' visitors in the Seychelles. But there they were, competing with Seychelles turtle doves, barred ground-doves, Madagascar and the endemic Seychelles fodies and even the Seychelles magpie robin, one of the most endangered birds in the world.

If you walk through the forest on Fregate or Cousin Island you may well come face to face with an enormous tortoise. It may be a relic of the endemic Seychelles giant tortoise but it is more likely to be one of those introduced from the island of Aldabra.

The seas around the Seychelles are rich in fish and support huge colonies of terns of various species. The lesser noddy is darker and has a longer beak than the brown noddy.

Although it is black and white and often carries its tail cocked up, the Seychelles magpie robin is, of course, neither a magpie nor a robin. It is a member of the thrush family and with its glossy black plumage and white wing-patches, looks like a sort of arboreal black guillemot. Despite its rather skulking habits and fondness for dark, gloomy places, it is not really a shy bird, but with only thirty or forty birds left in the world - and probably all of them on Fregate Island - it must be one of the rarest. It

was formerly found on several other islands in the Seychelles, and while nobody really knows the reason for its decline, serious studies are now being undertaken in order to try and find out.

The Seychelles fody is also a very rare bird, being confined to only three of the smaller islands in the Seychelles group. It is a small 'weaver-finch' type of bird, mainly dull greeny-brown in colour, though the male in breeding dress has a golden throat and forehead. It is locally called the 'toq-toq' from its call. The related Madagascar fody which has 'invaded' the Seychelles is a bolder, more aggressive

The Madagascar fody is locally called the cardinal and was introduced from Mauritius in the eighteenth century. It is commensal with man and readily adapts to take advantage of whatever is on offer. It will wait around restaurants until meal-times and descend on the tables to clean up plates - sometimes while you are still eating!

The endemic Seychelles fody seems a bit overawed by its introduced cousin. It is duller in colour and less 'pushy' in behaviour. Even its local name of 'toq toq' doesn't inspire. I photographed this pair in silhouette as they waited for their gaudy cousins to make room on the bird-table.

bird, and the males are most striking: bright red all over except for brownish wings and tail. The females are more like the endemic fodies in colour.

We only had two days on Fregate and I could easily have spent at least a week. There was much to see and we only 'scratched the surface'.

A walk through the plantation and the forest produced another endemic bird, the Seychelles blue pigeon, a spectacular bird with a blue and white plumage and a strange red 'comb' on its forehead. It is not uncommon on most of the main islands, but it tends to stay in the tree canopy and in spite of its gaudy plumage is not all that easy to see. Unfortunately it kept to the tops of the trees and didn't give me any chance of pictures.

Much easier to photograph were the giant tortoises which were lumbering around like tanks in the undergrowth. Some of them were said to be at least a hundred years old.

Indian mynahs were common and we saw several strange-looking mutants with bald yellow heads. Many sunbirds were flitting around, but I found them almost impossible to photograph with the equipment I had with me. I also realised that forest photography was fraught with problems I hadn't even considered, and was not at all well-equipped to deal with.

We flew back to Mahe and straight on to Praslin for a stay of a few days with the intention of taking day-trips to the smaller islands of Cousin and La Digue.

Cousin Island is a beautiful, uninhabited island which is run by the International Council for Bird Preservation. Access is by boat from Praslin. In the absence of any jetty we waded ashore, disturbing a flock of lesser noddy terns from the beach.

'Noddy' is the name given to a group of tropical terns whose plumage is like a negative of the more familiar shades of white body with a dark cap to the head. Noddies have a dark body with a white forehead or cap. Both lesser and greater (brown) noddies nest in large numbers on Cousin. They are tame and noisy and build seaweed nests in the casuarina trees along the shores.

Although there were thousands of lesser and hundreds of brown noddies on Cousin in October, it cannot be easy to assess the population size, because with no positive 'summer season' as we know it in the temperate zones, many birds can be found breeding almost throughout the year. The two noddies are fairly similar, but the lesser has a longer beak and the brown, as its name suggests, has a paler brown back.

Also nesting in large numbers was the white or fairy tern. This has to be the most elegant and beautiful of all the tern tribe. Snowy white in plumage, with a black beak and large jet black eyes, it lays a single egg on the bare branch of a tree, choosing a little hollow or crack in the bark so that the egg doesn't roll off. There it is incubated, and there the young sits until it is large enough to fly away.

Seychelles fody male displaying.

Tame and confiding, fairy terns have been known to nest on the rafter beams in some of the chalets occupied by tourists - it puts a new slant on having 'problems with your overheads'!

Accompanied by the warden we walked up the steep path to the rocky top of the island, seeing a few wedge-tailed shearwaters nesting almost out in the open like their relative the fulmar. By the path we saw a number of white-tailed tropic birds. They sat on their single egg and refused to move. Seen in flight they are the most graceful of birds, with a mainly white plumage and long, streaming tail-feathers, but at close quarters they are quite aggressive, jabbing with their big, sharp, yellow beak at anything within reach and swearing at passers-by.

The prize bird of Cousin Island is without doubt the Seychelles brush warbler. A rather unspectacular brown *Acrocephalus* warbler, it was thought to be in imminent danger of following the dodo into extinction until the ICBP bought the island and instituted a programme of saving and increasing its mangrove breeding habitat. As a result the warbler increased in numbers until by 1988 the population had built to the extent that it was decided that some birds could be caught and transported to the island of Aride, some twelve kilometres north, which is managed by the UK-based Royal Society for Nature Conservation. This was successfully accomplished and it will be most interesting to follow developments.

Cousin Island also has a small population of giant tortoises, including 'George' said to be 150 years old and one of the survivors of the endemic subspecies, the others having been introduced from the island of Aldabra which lies about a thousand kilometres away off the north of Madagascar.

Bridled and Brown Noddy and a white tern in the Seychelles.

Skinks and geckos were very numerous, and a walk along a forest track was accompanied by constant rustlings as these little reptiles scuttled off the path. I accidentally spilt some soft drink on the bench where we had lunch, and in a minute a dozen skinks had homed in and were lapping up the liquid.

Aride is another superb little island accessible by boat from Praslin. It is uninhabited apart from the RSNC wardens.

A considerable swell was breaking on the beach, so cameras were stowed in plastic bags and we surfed ashore in an inflatable in what is known as a 'wet landing'. It is great fun when the water temperature is thirty degrees Celsius.

It was obviously a 'tern island'. We saw large numbers on the crossing and thousands of lesser and brown noddies and fairy terns were breeding in the trees near the shore.

There were many rocky outcrops higher up, and here we found two more tern

One of the loveliest of all the tern family is the fairy tern (I am reluctant to accept its 'new' name of white tern). I had read about it and seen many pictures, and had come to look on this bird as the epitome of the tropical terns. They are so tame and confiding, so umcompromisingly ethereal and almost virginal that I found it difficult to accept that actually they are quite quarrelsome towards each other!

species nesting. Bridled and sooty terns have some similarities. Both are dark-backed, white-bodied terns with dark caps and a white forehead. But the sooty is 'blacker' above with a white forehead that extends only *to* the eye, while on the bridled the white forehead extends over and a little way *beyond* the eye.

At the peak of the breeding season there are said to be perhaps a quarter of a million sooty terns nesting on Aride, but now in October there were only a few hundred. Outside the breeding season, the terns are pelagic, ranging widely over the oceans. Bird Island in the Seychelles (which we didn't get to on this occasion) is said to have a colony of over two million!

We climbed up the easy slope to the top of the island, and found we were overlooking a sort of wooded cliff on the other side. Here hundreds of birds were wheeling and soaring and we realised with excitement that they were frigate birds.

There are five species of this large piratical sea-bird, and they are notoriously difficult to separate, but the warden told us this was a roosting place (they do not breed in the Seychelles) for mainly immature greater and lesser frigate birds, probably from the huge breeding colonies on Aldabra.

They are magnificent birds to watch in flight, soaring effortlessly on wings which can be over two metres from tip to tip. There is something primeval, almost reptilian about the narrow, sharply angled wings and twin-pointed tail. Apparently they neither walk nor swim, but spend their time either in the air or perched on a branch of a tree to roost.

Usually nesting in mixed colonies with lessers, the brown noddy is slightly bigger and shorter beaked. It is also distinctly brown over the mantle. Noddies build untidy seaweed nests in the casuarina trees near the shores.

The hillside was riddled with the burrows of Audubon's shearwaters and the warden pulled out a youngster to show us. Typical of young shearwaters, it was just a ball of grey down with a beak sticking out. Audubon's shearwaters range widely over tropical oceans, with apparently discrete populations in the Indian, Pacific and Atlantic Oceans. The taxonomy of the various populations is still not fully settled. We only saw the adult shearwaters at sea and they looked a bit like a small Manx shearwater, but with a brownish tinge to the upper parts.

Back on Praslin we spent half a day in the reserve of Vallée de Mai, which is probably of more interest to a botanist. It is the home of that most Freudian of plants, the coco-de-mer. Separate male and female trees grow side by side, and the female tree produces enormous double nuts which may weigh as much as eighteen kilogrammes each.

The fairy terns make no nest, but lay their single egg in a tiny hollow on a branch of a tree. There the young is hatched and fed until it is ready to fly.

The coco-de-mer grows only on Praslin and its neighbour Curieuse and has long been the subject of legends and superstitions. It is considered to have aphrodisiac properties, and some believe it to have been the original 'forbidden fruit' and that the Seychelles were the site of the Garden of Eden.

My interest in the Vallée de Mai was somewhat more prosaic. I was hoping to see the Seychelles black parrot, which has never been recorded from any island other than Praslin.

We had only brief glimpses of the parrot as it flew across gaps in the canopy, and with that I had to be content. We thought we heard their high-pitched whistles at times but, knowing that the mynahs on Praslin mimic the parrots accurately, we couldn't be sure. In fact the calls could also have been made by the Seychelles bulbul, a brown thrush-like bird with an orange-red beak which we saw feeding high up in the palms in several places.

We had one more day trip by boat before we left Praslin, and that was to the island of La Digue to try and see the black paradise flycatcher. Like so many of the Seychelles birds it is found only on the one island.

We hired bicycles and rode along the rutted road to the reserve. I hadn't ridden a bicycle in thirty years and was none too confidently negotiating the potholes, when suddenly an incredible-looking blue-black bird with a ridiculously long tail flew across the track - and I rode straight into the ditch!

Recovering my composure, if not much dignity, I followed the bird through the trees and came on a female (which lacks the long plumes and has a chestnut back and tail) which appeared to be nest-building almost above our heads. The pair ignored us completely and gave us superb views of yet another extremely rare endemic bird of the Seychelles.

By now I was enjoying the hot, sunny weather, but, alas, time was running out, and the last few days were spent back on Mahe. The Seychelles kestrel had so far eluded me, but I met an English birder while I was trying again to photograph waders in the harbour of Victoria, and he told me a pair had nested in one of the church towers in the town.

I found the church without too much trouble, and saw the spaces under the edge of the roof where the birds were said to have had their nest. Originally, the Seychelles kestrels nested in holes in the mountain crags but are said to have been ousted from that habitat by barn owls which were introduced to try and control the rat population. They found alternative sites under house roofs, but suffered because of a superstitious

White-tailed Tropic bird on its nest.

belief that they were omens of death. Today, the kestrel, if not endangered, is certainly one of the world's rarest birds of prey, with a population of only a few hundred.

After skulking around for half an hour I spotted a kestrel in a tree nearby. It was obviously a recently fledged bird, still with a few tufts of down adhering to its head, but of its parents there was no sign.

Fish featured largely in our diet during our stay, and being a keen fisherman I longed to get offshore and try for some of the bigger game fish. After counting the remaining rupees carefully, I spent the last free day in the company of a couple of young Seychellois who were going to an offshore reef to lift their fish-traps. Rods were set up and attached to gaudy plastic lures which were trolled some distance behind

White tern.

the boat. We watched for signs of bird activity, because terns and shearwaters congregate whenever small fish shoal near the surface of the sea, and the shoaling is often caused by predatory fish chasing the smaller fish upwards.

Sure enough, we were soon catching bonito, a fish in the tunny family which resembles a huge mackerel. They were around four or five kilogrammes in weight and were great sport. Then my reel screamed and I was into something much bigger. I played the fish for ten minutes without seeing a glimpse of it, then fifty metres away a huge fish, shining like a bar of silver, leaped into the air.

'Wahoo,' cried the Seychellois. I assumed this was the Creole equivalent to 'Tally-ho' or 'Thar she blows!' But no, it seemed to be the local name for the twenty kilo fish which was giving me a hard time, though later someone else called it a kingfish.

Anyway, whatever its name, it put up a noble fight before it was gaffed and brought on board, and I had my photograph taken with the catch after we landed back on the beach.

To me it was a fitting ending to a trip to the 'paradise islands'. We missed out on

The Seychelles black paradise flycatcher is found nowhere else in the world but on the island of La Digue. The male is dark blue with an incredibly long tail, while the female looks like an entirely different species, having a chestnut back and white front, and lacking the long tail-streamers.

The bridled tern nests on rat-free islands and lays its single egg on the ground. It might be confused with the sooty tern but is always paler backed, and the white forehead extends beyond the eye.

some of the rare birds. We didn't see the Seychelles scops owl, which is nocturnal and usually only seen if a tape-recording is played at night, nor did we get the little Seychelles white-eye, but I am not concerned. They will still be there when I go back again.

10 FALKLANDS REVISITED

On my first visit to the Falklands I was so taken by the sea-birds and the birds of prey that I didn't give the little birds as much attention as I ought.

Generally speaking, small birds are more difficult to photograph, because even though they may be quite approachable, you have to be that much closer in order to get a decent-sized image in the frame. They also tend to be much more rapid in their movements. An added problem for me was that I was working. It wouldn't be much fun for the group if the leader spent most of his time crawling around 'doing his own thing' while the rest watched.

But our parties are not encouraged to rush from place to place 'ticking off' birds and animals at high speed. We tend to amble and sit and watch quite a lot, and often enough birds will come up to inspect us.

After being weaned elephant seal pups lie around re-absorbing some of the fat laid on by their mother's very rich milk. They may indulge in 'play fights' in the shallow water but daren't venture farther out because of the danger of being caught and eaten by killer whales.

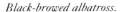

Black-browed albatross.

Sea-lion Island is - to my mind - an ideal size. It is big enough to offer a good variety of habitats, yet small enough that you can walk round it in a day. It has another advantage in not having any feral cats or rats, so small birds tend to be less afraid.

The owners of the island have long recognised the nutritional value of the tussac grass (which in some parts of the islands has been destroyed by over-grazing). Most of it is fenced off to protect it from sheep, though it can, of course, be selectively grazed when necessary. It also provides habitat for small birds, as well as for 'jackass' penguins and other creatures, like elephant seals.

The island is fairly low-lying and doesn't have the high craggy hills which suit species like red-backed hawks - but then no one island has everything the heart can desire!

Within ten minutes' walk of the lodge on Sea-lion Island there is a kilometre-long beach of white sand, and this beach is both breeding and moulting territory to a herd of huge elephant seals. They really are massive, a big bull can weigh as much as three and a half tonnes and be over five metres in length. Fortunately they are peaceable creatures (except with each other) and spend much of the breeding season just lying on the beach asleep.

Early in the season, when males are establishing territories and selecting favourite wives for their harems, there is much heavyweight wrestling and clashing of blubber as they try to slash at each other's necks.

It has to be admitted that the adult male southern elephant seal is a rather grotesque beast, with a large proboscis which is inflated and acts as a resonator for its belly-rumbling roars. Females and young are much prettier animals, although males soon show the beginnings of a wrinkled nose.

The seals' only enemies are killer whales, which can often be seen patrolling off the beaches. They usually hunt as a family party, with one large bull and several females and immatures. Woe betide any young elephant seal which may have strayed out into deep water, its life will be assured of a merciless but quick end.

When the elephant seals are moulting, the outer skin as well as the short hair is sloughed off in patches which lie around on the sand like discarded carpet samples. Whether to ease itching or to keep cool I am not sure, but the seals have the habit of throwing great 'flipperfuls' of sand over their backs as they lie dozing. This disturbs lots of small insects in the sand, which are pounced upon by tussac birds.

These starling look-alikes belong to a South American family called *Cincloides* and the Falkland race is restricted to the islands. The birds are plain brown in colour, but what they may lack in beauty they make up for by being absurdly tame. I have often had tussac birds pick crumbs from my hand, and a favourite occupation is to follow people walking on the beach, tripping over and around your feet on the outlook for insects. They will run over the bodies of sleeping seals, poking in the folds of skin for possible food, and they probably see people as mobile, upright elephant seals!

At the east end of the beach the sand turns to larger sea-rounded rocks and this is the favourite haunt of the house wren. Behaving in typical wren fashion by creeping mouse-like around and under boulders, it is in fact a *Troglodytes* like the familiar British wren and, like our Shetland wren, is an island sub-species. It is a plainer bird than ours, with less rusty barring on the plumage, and its song is lower pitched, with much shorter phrasing.

Birds (and people) living for a long time in isolated populations develop their own idiosyncratic way of communicating with their neighbours. This can be seen particularly well among the wrens who, once they have found an island, tend to stay there. I have listened to the wrens of St Kilda, the Faroe Islands, Fair Isle and Shetland, and I can detect consistent differences in phrasing, pitch and delivery of their songs. The Falkland Island house wren is different from all these, and I would expect that it is also different from its own nearest neighbours on Tierra del Fuego.

Like so many small birds, wrens are constantly on the move and very difficult to photograph well. One useful trick I often try is to get the bird interested by making squeaking noises with my lips. Sometimes - but only sometimes - the bird will be intrigued enough to stop briefly to listen, and that is when you take your photograph!

The tussac grass above the 'elephant beach' is a good place to look for the black-throated finch (which is really a bunting). The male is a cracker. Shades of blue/grey, yellow, black and white combine in a strong pattern. The female is more soberly dressed and looks like a female reed bunting with yellow on the tail and wing edgings. It is not particularly shy, but it is a restless bird, and flirts in and out of the tussac and long grass rather unpredictably.

A fairly similar species, the yellow-bridled finch, occurs in southern South America, and when Charles Darwin visited the Falkland Islands in 1841 he reported

Nature 'red in tooth and claw' can sometimes by witnessed off the beaches of the Falklands as killer whales grab unwary seals. Male killers can be ten metres long and are identified by the high dorsal fin.

This beautiful little black-throated finch is restricted to the southern tip of South America with an endemic race in the Falkland Islands. The males are very distinctive with their dark 'mask' but the females are brown streaked and more bunting-like.

that it too was common, remarking that 'it more commonly frequents the higher parts of the hills'. Since that time there have been very few records and no sightings have been recorded in the last thirty years.

Walk west along the shores from 'elephant beach' and you will eventually come to some low cliffs. You could walk along the rocks below the cliffs, but it is not advised, because this the territory of the colony of southern sea-lions from which the island takes its name. Although not quite as large as the elephant seals, males are about two metres in length and weigh over three hundred kilogrammes. What they lack in size, they more than make up for by being belligerent and *much* more agile.

They too operate the harem principle, the males gathering a dozen or so females each - depending how well they can fight. Males from adjoining territories are constantly on the alert, roaring and swearing at rivals, and bloody battles are not

Short-eared owls are very widely distributed, being found in both hemispheres, and the Falkland birds have been described as a separate race. They breed in the long grass, often near tussac paddocks and some feed on the night-flying grey-backed storm petrels.

uncommon. Younger bulls sometimes get ideas 'above their station' and try to steal an attractive female from an older bull. Then all hell is let loose.

Sea-lions can use their hind flippers as 'legs', which enables them to move with considerable speed on land. A big 'beachmaster' will certainly charge towards anyone approaching his harem, and I for one have no wish to prove whether he would actually attack.

The cliffs backing the sea-lion's territory are six or more metres in height, and this makes an admirable viewpoint from which to watch the activity in the colony. In late summer there will be lots of attractive, very dark brown pups. Groups of them will play 'tag' in the rock pools or chase each other over the rocks. The sleek, fawn-coloured females will be lying about sleeping or suckling young. The males, with their massive manes (which are mostly blubber) appear to doze, but are always ready to sit up and roar defiance at any real (or imagined) threat to their dominance.

The third member of the pinnipeds (which means 'fin-footed') to breed in the Falklands is the South American fur seal. It breeds on the more remote islands such as New Island, which are not so readily accessible to visiting groups. The fur seal is about half the size of the sea-lion, and even more agile. Apart from having more pointed noses, they have a superficial resemblance to their larger relatives.

Beyond the territory of the sea-lions is a large, fenced-off area of tussac interspersed with various grasses, and this is good habitat for several species of birds. Common or Magellan snipe love the cover of the longer grass and are so wonderfully camouflaged that unless they fly or run off, they are very difficult to spot. There is no full agreement about the identity of this snipe. Some claim it is a race of the European snipe *Gallinago gallinago*. Others say it is *Gallinago paraguaiae*, the Magellan snipe. The snipe, of course, continues to live its life oblivious to the arguments.

It has a paler, less contrasty plumage than our northern type and, like many Falkland birds, is exceptionally tame. It will feed or preen out in the open, at times allowing a photographer to approach as close as two metres or so.

Another bird of the tussac paddock is the short-eared owl, *Asio flammeus*, a bird which is well distributed over both hemispheres. The Falkland bird looks similar to the ones which haunt the moors of Iceland, Scotland and Orkney, but taxonomists have ascribed it to a local race and called it *A. f. sandfordi*. It seems less prone to hunting in broad daylight than our northern bird, but this is possibly because its chief prey are birds which are active at night. It is believed to live mainly on the small storm petrels and prions which only come in to land after darkness has fallen, but it is also known to feed on the camel-crickets which live in the tussac grass.

One (or more) owls have a habit of coming round the lodge on Sea-lion Island just after dusk, probably seeking out the large moths which are attracted to the lighted windows.

By day they roost in the tussac grass, where their cryptic plumage blends in very well among the brown and green stems. It takes a keen eye to spot an owl among the grass, and one day while we were walking through the long grass, one of the party suddenly said 'Shhh!' and pointed. There was a short-eared owl on the ground with only its head and shoulders visible through the waving grass. It was perhaps about twelve metres away, and was staring at us with its round orange eyes.

At this point I decided to apply the only strategy I knew which would, I hoped, allow everyone who was equipped to take photographs a chance of a picture. I waved the party together, and all took such photographs as their equipment would allow, from that position. Then we all moved slowly forward a few metres, stopped and again took photographs. Then when everyone was satisfied they had got all they could, we moved forward again - pushing our luck this time. Still the owl didn't move, but continued to stare at us fixedly.

We got to about four metres from the bird, stopped and there was no sound but the clicking of camera shutters. Then we signalled mutely that we had got all we could hope for, and we backed off as quietly as we could and left the bird in peace.

On one of my trips to the Falklands I was due to take two groups round one after the other, and I found myself with a couple of days to spare between the two. I specially wished to see a breeding colony of black-browed albatross, so with the help of friends it was arranged that I should fly out to Saunders Island.

I was greeted with the typical unpretentious warmth of islanders, and invited to make myself at home with one of the two families on the island.

I went for a walk along the cliffs nearby after being told that a hawk usually nested there. I found other things to photograph, including some clumps of the lovely 'lady's slipper', a *Calceolaria* endemic to the islands. The 'diddle-dee' berries were just beginning to appear, and on a slope near the cliff edge there was a scarlet carpet of berries which I wished to use as a foreground to a general scene.

I had taken one shot and was angling for another when I heard the unmistakable screech of a bird of prey. I looked round and there was a beautiful female red-backed hawk soaring over the cliff edge. Conditions were perfect, with the sun shining in a blue sky, and I quickly changed to a telephoto lens. The bird continued to soar quite near and I took a series of photographs.

The hawk eventually landed on the hillside and continued to call occasionally. I knew there had to be a nest nearby. I walked a few metres further, peered over the cliff and there it was. Two nearly full-grown young hawks stood on a platform of sticks and grass, a mere six metres away on a small ledge in the cliff. They showed only curiosity as I set up my tripod and took more photographs.

Then, to complete the family, the male came flying along clutching some small food offering in his talons - through binoculars it looked like the remains of a snipe. He veered off when he saw me squatting on the cliff edge, but came soaring back and to my delight perched not six metres away.

This was almost too good to be true. I re-positioned my tripod and took pictures of the grey-backed male (only the female has a red back) as he stood there so unconcerned at my presence.

Mindful of the instructions I had been given about lunch - that there was 'half a sheep in the oven' - I left the birds to feed their young, and hurried back to the house to quell my own hunger pangs, delighted about the pictures I hoped were 'in the can'.

I have two lasting memories of that afternoon: one is of my first encounter, on its breeding grounds, with that beautiful bird, the black-browed albatross. The other is still awe at where a Landrover can be persuaded to go!

The path - if it can be called that - to the colony was up a steep hillside, over a rock ridge more suited to a mountaineering training-ground, down the slope at the other side, and into the sea to cross the mouth of a river. The final assault was (I swear!) a forty-five degree slope close enough to a cliff to disturb parties of rockhopper penguins as they made their way to their nests. But it was all very much worth it.

overleaf: *Intelligent, mobile and generally good-natured, the southern sea-lions belong to the* Otariid *group of seals (i.e. they have external ear-flaps). Young animals are playful and sometimes friendly towards humans, but beware adult bulls in the breeding season. They are very large animals weighing up to 300 kg and bad-tempered in defence of their harem. This mother and yearling pup were photographed at Cape Bougainville in the north part of East Falkland.*

The red-backed hawk is a member of the Buteo *family, as is our buzzard. Only the females have a red back; this is a male bird. They are very approachable, as are most of the Falklands birds. Like many birds of prey they are very vocal if you encroach on a breeding territory, but if you sit still for a bit they will often perch nearby and allow a photograph - as this one did.*

The Antarctic skua looks quite similar to our Shetland bonxie and has the same piratical habits. It often nests close to rockhopper penguin colonies and preys on their eggs and young. It is very fierce in defence of its own nest and will attack in no uncertain manner anyone who approaches.

The black-browed albatross is strictly a southern hemisphere bird, but like all albatrosses away from the breeding-grounds it wanders widely over the oceans. Occasionally a few individuals wander too far north and, presumably, get a bit lost. They may then attach themselves to the only big sea-bird in the north which vaguely resembles an albatross in shape and size, in this case the gannet.

Three instances of this come to mind. There was the famous 'súlukongur' (king of the gannets) which stayed on the island of Mykines in Faroe for thirty-four years (and which I wrote about in an earlier chapter). Another was found to have joined the gannets on the Bass Rock in the Firth of Forth one season, and it may have been the same bird which subsequently turned up among the gannets on Hermaness in Shetland. This one stayed around for fifteen years, always using the same ledge, where it even built a nest. Whether it was male or female nobody knows - certainly no egg was ever seen.

Needless to say it became something of a celebrity bird in Shetland, and many is the party of people I have taken across to Saito, to peer over the two hundred metre cliff at this lonely albatross sitting on its nest halfway down the cliff.

So to see an albatross in its 'real home' had long been an ambition of mine.

The black-browed albatross is one of the most numerous and widely distributed of all the albatrosses, breeding on islands in all the oceans south of about sixty-five degrees. In the Falklands the largest colony is on Bêauchene Island, the most southerly outlier, where it is reckoned about 150,000 nest. There is a large colony on the Jason Islands and smaller numbers on other islands off the West Falkland coast such as New Island, Saunders Island, West Point Island and Kepple Island. Nesting either on steep slopes or in grassy cliffs, they build a large nest of mud and guano, which is added to each year until it can be fifty centimetres in height.

Although the black-browed albatross does have a 'scowling' look, due to the black line through the eye which gives the bird its name, they are lovely gentle characters. Completely unafraid of man, they come and go about their business as if you weren't there. I was totally engrossed by them, and was startled back to reality by the reminder that it was time we were heading back to the settlement and supper.

Carcass Island is another super place to visit, particularly for smaller birds, as there are neither cats nor rats to predate them. It was here that I got to grips (in the photographic sense) with several of the passerines with which, so far, I hadn't had much luck.

Carcass Island was named after HMS 'Carcass', a ship of the Royal Navy, and only one family lives on the island. Their house is surrounded by a grove of trees, mainly of Monterey cypress. This is an introduced species which grows particularly well in the Falklands, which have no native trees. The path down from the house to the beach is partly 'roofed' by cypress branches, and at one point both branches and path are liberally splashed by droppings from a colony of black-crowned night-herons.

Locally called 'quarks' from the hoarse call, the species is widespread in North and South America, and also in Africa and southern Europe. The Falkland race *cyanocephalus* is smaller and darker than most mainland birds. Normally they nest in tussac clumps, often on cliffs, but here they had found a suitable home in the *Macrocarpa* trees. They were a beautiful and unusual 'garden bird' even if they did make the path a little messy!

Naturally I spent some time with the quarks, and also got some pictures of the Falkland thrushes which came along to see what I was up to. This bird is endemic to the islands, its 'proper' name being *Turdus falklandii*. It is a common resident round the settlements, and also in the tussac grass, particularly where this backs on to boulder beaches. It is blackbird-like in size and behaviour, and a bit like a female blackbird in colour. The sexes differ only a little - the male is usually darker around the head. Both have yellow bills and yellow/brown legs.

The thrush is tame enough, if a little suspicious, and it was on Carcass that I had the time to wait until the birds settled down and decided I was probably harmless.

The sun was shining and for once there was little wind. I parked myself on a log with my back against a corrugated iron shed and waited to see what might turn up. The beach in front of me was shingly with ridges of flat rocks here and there. Both Magellan and blackish oystercatchers were feeding along the tideline, the Magellans more flighty and noisy, occasionally taking wing in a bunch and flying round with their high-pitched 'pee pee pee' call. Most individuals had a very slight difference in pitch which together made a wonderfully discordant sound.

Parties of flightless steamer ducks were feeding and quarrelling noisily along the edge of the kelp-beds, their loud *cheeroo, cheeroo* echoing across the bay. A small flock of Patagonian crested duck, locally called 'grey duck', were quietly feeding in a rock pool, while a pair of kelp geese were escorting a brood of goslings down the beach towards the sea.

This activity was being watched intently by an Antarctic skua which was standing on a boulder, no doubt assessing its chance of grabbing a gosling before being attacked by the white gander.

A small party of speckled teal came flying in from the sea and settled on a pool of fresh water formed by the tiny stream which flowed down past the house. They didn't appear to have seen me and began to bathe vigorously, while I eased myself slowly round and focused my camera for a picture.

A couple of jackass penguins which had been making their way up from the sea suddenly spotted me and stopped, twisting their heads comically almost upside down as they tried to puzzle out what I was doing. They then panicked a bit and scuttled on as fast as their short legs could move, to disappear into the undergrowth below the trees in the garden.

If I had any doubts as to what they were doing in the garden they were dispelled at dawn next morning. A cacophony of braying like a herd of demented donkeys came from nesting burrows, one of them right outside my bedroom window!

There was a flicker of wings and a little grey bird with a darker head settled on a stone in front of me. It flicked its wings and tail and examined me with its bright eye as I lined up the camera. At the 'click' of the shutter it was off again, but I felt sure I had got a useful picture.

It was a dark-faced ground-tyrant, one of a group of South American birds called tyrant-flycatchers. It is fairly common in the Falklands, often seen in the stone runs and along the shores. In its behaviour and habits it reminds me of our wheatear, having the same flirting and bobbing actions. Its local names are 'news-bird' or 'blue-bird' and while neither are particularly apt names, they are better than the clumsy 'book name' of dark-faced ground-tyrant! It was called 'news-bird' because of the

right: *It was the black-browed albatross more than any other bird which first attracted me to visit the Falkland Islands. They are such gentle giants, sitting unconcernedly on their built-up nests and ignoring the presence of humans nearby. They are even more impressive in flight on wings which are about 240 cm from tip to tip.*

far right: *The black-crowned night heron is another species with a wide distribution covering North and South America as well as Africa. The race breeding widely in Falkland is darker and a little smaller than most. Its favourite breeding-place is on tussac-covered cliff faces, but a colony is estab-lished in the* Macrocarpa *trees in the settlement on Carcass Island where I took this photograph. It lays three or four eggs on a sort of platform nest and the fledged young are dark brown flecked with buff. It is called 'quark' locally from its harsh call.*

right: *The turkey vulture performs a useful service in clearing up carcasses of dead sheep and the like. Again Falkland birds are a race of a more widespread species. They often nest under tussac stools, usually laying two whitish eggs in a mere scrape in the ground. They have a characteristic soaring flight.*

Black-necked swan.

belief that if the bird came near to the house - especially if it fluttered in front of a window - it foretold the arrival of news from far away.

A shadow overhead made me look up, and I nearly dropped my camera as a turkey vulture settled on the ridge of the shed above me. It held its huge wings outspread like some heraldic symbol, as it examined me with its piercing eyes, set in a head of naked red skin. The jet-black plumage, the naked red head and the large, hooked, cream-coloured beak all added up to a menacing-looking ensemble. I learned afterwards that it too was nesting in the garden.

As I was about to leave the log by the shed which had been so productive photographically, I heard a snatch of birdsong apparently coming from a patch of long grass and reeds near the little stream. I sneaked up as quietly as I could and sat down on the bank, but there was no sign of the songster. After a while I tried my 'squeaking trick' and was immediately answered by a churring from within the patch of tangled grass.

I kept silent for a moment, and then there was a twitching of the grass stems and a tiny, brown-streaked, warbler-like bird showed itself briefly. So that was it! The bird I had looked for in vain on my first trip - the grass wren. It was very elusive indeed, and extremely reluctant to show itself in the open. I 'squeaked' until my mouth was dry, but it had got wise to that trick.

I did get a couple of 'snatch shots' before giving up and going for a walk up through the paddocks beyond the house.

The hen-run produced several birds - apart from the chickens. There were several news-birds flitting about and fly-catching from the posts of the enclosure. Several black-throated finches flew off when I approached, and to my delight a pair of black-chinned siskins with them settled on the wire of the run for long enough to let me take a few shots.

This is another native of the southern part of South America which is widespread, though nowhere plentiful, in the Falklands. It is a much yellower bird than the European siskin, with unstreaked yellow underparts. It likes the tree plantations but can also be seen in the tussac in places.

There was one other stunning bird which had so far evaded my attempts to get a good picture, and that was the long-tailed meadowlark, sometimes called military starling.

Like starlings it tends to forage over the fields in small squabbling parties - even sounding a bit like starlings. It is only when one turns round and shows its brilliant scarlet front that you are reminded that here is another South American species with an outpost in the Falklands.

I had tried stalking them in other islands without much success, but here on Carcass I had time to try other tactics. They, too, were attracted to the hen-run, so I just made myself as comfortable and unobtrusive as possible and waited. It wasn't too long before a trio came flying along and perched on the wires without appearing to notice my presence. One perched on the wire above me so near I couldn't focus the lens on it. I think it is a real cracker of a bird!

My two days on Carcass passed all too quickly. I explored as much of the coast as was possible, enjoying the birds and animals and the unspoiled island scenery. Being escorted to the airstrip by two beautiful young island lasses on horseback was a nice way to end the trip.

I hope to get back to the Falklands as often as possible. I feel an empathy with the islands which in some ways are like Shetland, yet in others very different. I enjoy the space and the unspoiled nature of it all, the honest island people living in a crime-free society. I am impressed by their obvious respect for the natural world, which is interlinked with their own lives in a way city-dwellers can never really know.

But perfection is only an ideal. Their wealth of sea-birds and mammals is only made possible by a sea rich in food, and that resource is already under pressure from the demands of the over-populated world. Man has not yet learned to take heed of previous mistakes - I wonder if he ever will. . .

No visitor to the Falklands can fail to be impressed by the long-tailed meadowlark. They behave and even sound a bit like starlings (to which they are related), but the brilliant red breast is almost startling in its intensity. They are familiar birds round settlements nesting in hidden crevices under tussac or gorse bushes.

As its name suggests the South American fur seal has its main breeding grounds on the coasts and islands off South America. There are also colonies on some of the more rocky outlying islands in the Falklands. Hunting - mainly during the last century - threatened to exterminate some populations, but there are welcome indications of recovery in places.

From its tail to its distinctively pointed nose, an adult male fur seal is about two metres in length. Most pups are born on rocky cliff ledges in early December.

11 THE YEAR'S END

I get back from the Falklands in mid-December all tanned by the sun and wind of the southern summer, to find that apart from the longer hours of darkness, little has changed. The weather is still in the run of mild south-westerlies which has characterised the early winter period for a number of years.

After a day of catching up on news and mail and attending to a few urgent things, I set out next morning to see what is going on among the birds and beasts of my 'patch'. It is evident that the continuing mild weather has encouraged some birds to stay on in Shetland. My own front garden and the neighbour's cabbage patch have over a dozen blackbirds, most in their first winter plumage of sooty black and with black beaks. Only a couple of males have the bright yellow beak which denotes adulthood. Blackbirds are a good example of a bird which is migratory in the northern part of its range and resident in the milder southerly part.

Every year in late October or November we get a flood of Scandinavian blackbirds

It is only just over a hundred years since blackbirds first colonised Shetland, but now they are familiar 'garden' birds, nesting in outhouses or bushes. Many Scandinavian migrant blackbirds also pass through, but our birds are resident and readily take advantage of 'hand outs' in hard weather.

passing through Shetland, and it appears that our resident birds take a dim view of this invasion. I have seen many a skirmish as 'our' birds defend their territories and 'possession being nine-tenths of the law' certainly applies, as the resident bird always seem to come off best.

With the wind from the south, the gulls waiting for the salmon feeding to start are sitting in the park below my house where it is more sheltered. There are no 'strangers' among them that I can detect, but the near-albino herring gull, which normally lives a couple of kilometres north of here, has joined the party. This bird, now an adult, has been known to me for some years, and has given rise to a number of false reports of glaucous, Iceland or even of ivory gulls. It is white all over with only the palest of grey smudges on the back, while the wing-tips show only pale 'shadows' of the normal herring gull's black markings.

Jill Merlin.

I don't see the small flock of twite on the potato field until they fly off, but I pick up the slightly harsher note of redpoll among them. A cock chaffinch flies up at the same time, but lands on the fence and scolds with his 'pink pink' call. Then a female also appears from the potato field and together they fly off.

There is nothing round the pier except a bedraggled immature shag hanging its wings out to dry, and a few hooded crows and starlings scrounging for titbits in the salmon boats. More gulls are roosting on the school playing-field, this time with a few common gulls and a couple of black-headed gulls. A redshank rises up with its usual alarmed yelping when I stop the car to scan over the gulls, but three curlew at the far side merely stop probing the ground while they check that the redshank is only panicking again.

A small bird flies from the salmonberry hedge near Hillend as I pass, and the flight pattern suggests reed bunting. I pull in quickly and pick up the bird again with my glasses as it lands on a fence post. It is a reed bunting, a female (or young) and I suspect it is probably locally bred. My sister, who lives nearby, has seen and heard a male bird singing during the summer around the *Juncus* rushes in the wet meadow.

Out of the village and on to the main road; not far from the junction a party of ravens, hooded crows and a single black-backed gull get up from the remains of a sheep which is lying in the roadside ditch. No doubt the victim of a vehicle accident, and sadly one which doesn't raise much comment locally, although visitors are likely to be upset at times.

Moving on to Whalfirth, I stop at my usual vantage-point overlooking the sheltered waters of the voe. I wind down the window and survey the scene.

Three herons are immediately obvious, hunched up in the lee of a peaty bank, looking as dejected as only herons can. Judging by the dark grey of their necks they are young birds born this year, perhaps the offspring of the birds I saw in the same place last January - who knows? A fourth is standing in the shallows, long neck outstretched as it waits for some unsuspecting small fish to swim past.

There isn't much going on at the dump, just a few hoodies and starlings perched on the high mesh fence which prevents light materials from blowing all over the countryside.

I stop when I come over the hill beyond the loch of Lungawater and watch an oil-tanker making her sedate way in towards the entrance to the oil port of Sullom Voe, her 'brood' of red tugs looking like ducklings as they guide the huge ship in through the deep entrance channel.

In Westsandwick, there are a few fieldfares and redwings and more blackbirds feeding on the black earth disturbed by the recent lifting of the potato crop, and a careful scan with the binoculars reveals a party of twite and a couple of chaffinch. A small flock of lapwing and a few curlew are also feeding on the fields, but there is no sign of the expected flock of golden plover.

I am counting a group of rock doves which are feeding on the stubble when I hear the plovers overhead, giving their lovely, liquid piping calls as they glide in to land in a field nearby. Their black fronts all gone, they are now in full winter plumage, and I try to look hard at each individual in the hope that they might have been joined by one of their slimmer, longer-legged relatives from North America or Asia.

The swans have gone from the little loch now, probably having grazed out the modest amount of underwater vegetation, and only a couple of mallard are up-ending in the shallows.

The sky darkens as a rain shower spatters the windscreen and I turn and head for home. As I come over the hill my eye is caught by a movement in a rainwater pool near the roadside, and I pull off the road. But it is only a party of starlings bathing vigorously in the shallow puddle. They are chattering away among themselves as usual, when one suddenly gives its 'Look out, danger!' call, and the group freezes.

overleaf, left: *Our only resident member of the finch family is the twite. In summer it breeds sparingly but widely, often in sea cliffs, but also on heather hillsides or in gardens. It is a fairly unobtrusive bird, but a small winter flock perched in a row on a fence and all singing their little 'twangy' song is a charming sight.*

overleaf, right: *Habitat destruction, pollution and people pressure
have all helped to reduce or
eliminate otter populations in
many former British and
European haunts. Remote,
undisturbed - often coastal - areas
of the north and west of Britain
are now the best bet for a sighting
of this lovely mammal.*

*In Shetland, with its maze of
inlets and streams, the otter is still
common and, especially in winter
and spring, can be seen out fishing
along the shores at any time of day.*

I look round and sure enough, there is a merlin winging its way low along the hillside, no doubt on the outlook for a meal. As it crosses the road it suddenly sweeps upwards and perches on the 'cross-trees' of a power pole.

It is near enough that I can see the plumage details and identify it as a female, probably a young bird of the year which has been reared in an old crow's nest somewhere on a hillside in the interior of the island.

In Iceland and the Faroes the merlin is still called by its old Norse name of 'smyril', but this name no longer appears to be known in Shetland. But a number of place names such as Smirlees Hill, Smirlees Dale and Smirla Water suggest that the name was formerly in use here, and the fact that most of them are still in merlin territories suggests that this dashing little falcon has been around a long, long time!

I have often pondered over bird names and where they originated. Many are obviously constructed by specialist ornithologists. Names like 'dark-faced ground-tyrant' or 'broad-tailed paradise whydah' could hardly have come from any other source! But at least they do conjure up some image of what the bird might look like.

If you know nothing about birds, however, it would be very difficult to picture an 'Andalusian hemipode' or a 'striated caracara', and what would you say if someone rang your doorbell to tell you there was a boat-tailed grackle in your garden? Local names are often apt and to the point, though they can be corrupted over the years. Who would have guessed that the name 'wheatear' originated as the Old English name 'white-arse' - which makes sense for this bird with its flashing white rump.

Another bird to have suffered a name change is the fulmar. The name was originally 'foul-maa' which means 'stinking gull', quite apt for this bird which pukes up foul-smelling oil from its stomach.

Fulmar.

144

The name 'maa' for gull is of Norse origin and is still in common use in Shetland, but the name we have for the fulmar is 'mally'. Why is this? Well, the most likely explanation is that the fulmar has only been known in Shetland for just over a hundred years, and so didn't have a 'Norse-derived' name locally. But the bird was recognised by seafarers as a 'mollymauk' or 'molly', the common 'sea name' for any of the small albatrosses or petrels. It was a simple transition to 'mally', the name by which the bird is known in Shetland to this day.

Most well-known Shetland birds have local names, many of which originated in the days when the Old Norse language was common to Scandinavia, Denmark, Shetland, Orkney, Faroe and Iceland. Tystie, our name for the black guillemot, is an obvious one, and is known also to most British birders. In Iceland it is 'teista', in Faroe 'teisti' and so on with slight variations until in Germany it is 'gryllteiste'.

There are many such examples, but also some anomalies; why, for instance, is the Shetland name for some natural objects more akin to the Latin or scientific names? Take the bird called in English 'great northern diver', the scientific name of which is *Gavia immer*. The common Shetland name is 'immer goose'.

Could the connection be through Karl von Linné, the biologist who was the 'father' of the scientific classification of birds and other natural subjects? He was a native of Sweden, one of the Scandinavian countries. Perhaps a linguist who reads this will tell me.

Another one which puzzled me was the Shetland name for the little auk, which is 'rotchie'. This didn't seem to have any parallels in the Scandinavian languages. Then I read a book based on the diaries of a ship's surgeon who had spent the winter of 1866/7 in the Greenland sea. His ship, the Hull whaler 'Diana', got trapped in the ice and was forced to spend the winter frozen in. He spoke of the relief felt by those of the crew had survived the cold and the scurvy, when a flock of 'roaches' flew past. This indicated that the break-up of the ice was imminent.

So is the name 'rotchie' another 'sailor's name', like 'mally', or is it possibly an Inuit name? Certainly the whaling crews were familiar with both little auks and Eskimos during the many seasons they spent hunting the whale, and it would not be surprising if the name had become familiar in Shetland.

My great-great-grandfather spent thirty-six seasons at the Greenland whaling, and when chided by a cousin that 'Surely you are not going back to the whaling again' he replied, 'I'll be going back as long as I am able to break a ship's biscuit!' Jocky went back next season, but slipped between the ship and the ice while trying to 'cut a dock' and was badly crushed. He survived to get back home to his family, but never fully recovered from his injuries and died a few months later.

Many bird names are onomatopoeic, that is they describe the bird's call in words; hoopoe, whip-poor-will, toq-toq, caracara, kittiwake and cuckoo are a few obvious ones.

A Shetland name in this category is 'caloo'. This is our name for the long-tailed duck, a bird which spends its summer on the Arctic tundra, and then flies down to Shetland, Orkney and northern Scotland, where it spends the winter in coastal waters. As with many sea-ducks its plumage is at its best in winter when it probably does most of its courting. It is at this time also that it is most vocal.

During the Shetland winter, calm days are not all that frequent, but are made more enjoyable if a flock of long-tailed duck are wintering nearby. The lovely yodelling

Our most familiar 'seagull' the herring gull is probably resident, although we may get some immigrants in winter. A typical survivor, the herring gull will take advantage of whatever it can find that is edible. In winter especially it forages on the shores at low tide, picking up molluscs and crabs. It has learnt the trick of breaking open mussel shells by dropping them from a height on to the rocks.

Although the chaffinch is a familiar bird on the mainland areas of Britain, it is unlikely that the resident British chaffinches ever visit Shetland. Our birds are passage migrants from Scandinavia which will overwinter here in suitable areas if the weather is mild.

The greatest opportunist of them all, the hooded crow, is an all too familiar bird in the opinion of many people. Clever and mischievous, it is a thief, a scavenger and a killer all rolled in one. In spite of it all, I have a sneaking regard for its abilities in the art of survival.

The Shetland starling population is not large enough to cause any serious problems to humans. Even their roosting sites are generally well out of the way in sea caves.

Snow bunting flock in winter.

'cal-cal-caloo' of the drakes carries a kilometre across the water, the perfect embellishment to a fine winter day.

I love the Faroese name for the wren. They call it 'músabrooir' which means 'brother to the mouse'!

> Hail to thee, blithe spirit!
> Bird thou never wert
> That from heaven or near it
> Pourest thy full heart
> In profuse strains of unpremeditated art.

Those are the opening lines of Shelley's poem *To a Skylark* which, as a little boy, I had to learn to recite in school. I could scarcely speak English, far less understand the meaning of 'profuse strains of unpremeditated art', but neither did I ever forget the lines. The skylark was almost bound to inspire poetic phrases, soaring heavenward, pouring out its welcome to the spring when other birds - perhaps wisely - remain silent and suspicious.

In Shetland the skylark is known by at least two other names: one is 'lav' rock, which appears to be Scottish in origin. Certainly Robbie Burns uses it in more than one of his poems. The other is 'ledyin' and was the name I knew before I had even heard of 'skylark'.

I have seen this name explained as 'lady's hen' or even 'Our Lady's hen, suggesting a religious origin, but I think a more likely explanation lies with the old Norse name for a 'high vantage point', which is 'ledi'. The name still exists in Shetland as a place name for a piece of high ground: the 'Ledi of Basta' and the 'Lediens of Westsandwick', for example. In both places the 'profuse strains of unpremeditated art' can still be heard.

In the southern part of Shetland the local name for the corn bunting was the 'trussi laverock' which means 'untidy skylark'; in Orkney the same bird is called 'skitterbroiltie'! We used to call it the 'docken sparrow', and I mourn the demise of the corn bunting, a harmless bird which just couldn't cope with changing circumstances.

There is no 'hard' evidence to prove what caused the decline and extinction of corn bunting, but I suspect it had to do with changes in crofting and farming practices, in particular the increased use of seed oats which were bought already 'dressed' with pesticides.

I rouse myself from my thoughts, shivering a bit as I start up the car and turn on the heater. The meagre winter daylight has already begun to fade and I head back home. I have seen nothing unusual, but neither is there anything noticeably missing. Is the satisfying feeling of continuity perhaps a subconscious attempt to reassure myself that all is well with the world and its wildlife?

In the preceding chapters I have roamed over a lot of ground from the Arctic almost to the Antarctic. I have seen a great many birds and animals, and something of how they cope with a wide variety of climatic conditions. I have also seen something of how people live in other islands. My impression is that the more remote from so-called civilisation, the greater is the need to live off the land but, perhaps paradoxically, there is also more sympathy for the wildlife which shares that environment. If an Eskimo didn't kill seals he would die, and if an Eskimo killed all his seals he would die. There is a natural balance which is vitally important, and it is usually commercial interests which throw that balance out of step.

I realise that in my wanderings, I have only lifted a corner of the blanket and had a peek underneath. If I have shown a bias towards islands I can only admit it. I am island-bred and island-born. I find jungles claustrophobic, mountains picturesque but untouchable, and the huge deserts and plains incomprehensible. Much as I love the sea I am not of the stuff from which 'around the world alone' sailors are made.

Shetland wren.

I would probably be very bored with my own company. I do love the intimacy of the little islands and shorelines in all their many moods; the rhythms and continuity of the seasons and the way wild things have adapted to use every available niche - and will continue to do so if we give them half a chance.

I am not really a seeker after great truths, I do not expect to have a blinding flash of revelation and from then on to understand how and why the world works as it does. To my regret I am not really a fighter for 'great causes'. There are so many sides to every argument, and I find it depressingly easy to be swayed by someone else's point of view. I like to think I have an open mind but I suppose I am really a pragmatist at heart. My contact with the realities of the natural world supplies a lot of the answers I cannot find (or do not know how to look for) in a spiritual sense.

I have been privileged to see some of the lovely, unspoiled places left in this overcrowded world of ours, together with a selection of the birds, beasts and flowers which have been in existence since long before man came to exercise his 'dominion over the fowls of the air and the fishes in the sea. . .'
Christians believe this to be a God-given right, but I cannot help wondering if perhaps there might have been a transcription error and that God really meant 'responsibility'. If we could accept and live by that, the world might be a better place.

The Arctic-breeding turnstone is really widespread in winter. I have seen them on hotel bird-tables in the Seychelles, working the tidelines of an English beach and turning over cowpats in a Shetland field. This birds in its winter plumage seems to be examining the possibilities in another bird's dropping!

In winter when small birds are very scarce up on the Shetland hills, the merlin usually leaves for more productive feeding grounds. A few may stay on for a while and harry the migrants and small birds round the crofts. A merlin and a sparrow found drowned together in a water butt told a sad story of a chase that ended in disaster.

I hope you have enjoyed this book, There is a lot of environmental doom and gloom about, and while some of it is no doubt justified, I think it is vitally important to keep a sense of proportion. I have a lot of belief in the ability of mother nature to sort things out when it really becomes necessary.